THE ISLANDS SERIES

THE HOLY ISLAND OF LINDISFARNE AND THE FARNE ISLANDS

THE ISLANDS SERIES

Achill
The Åland Islands
Alderney
The Aran Islands
The Isle of Arran
The Island of Bute
Canary Islands: Fuerteventura
Cape Breton Island
Corsica
Cyprus
*Dominica
The Falkland Islands
*Gotland
Grand Bahama
Harris and Lewis
The Isle of Mull
Jamaica
Jersey
Lundy
The Maltese Islands
Mauritius
*Minorca
Orkney
*Puerto Rico
Rhodes
The Ryukyu Islands

St Kilda and Other Hebridean
   Islands
*Sardinia
The Isles of Scilly
*The Seychelles
Shetland
*Sicily
*Singapore
Skye
*The Solomon Islands
Staffa
Tasmania
Uists and Bara
Vancouver Island

In preparation
Colonsay and Oronsay
Fiji
Guadeloupe
Guernsey
The Six Inner Hebrides
Islay
Sark
Tahiti
Tobago
Tonga
Valentia

*Published in the United States by Stackpole
All other titles published in the United States by David & Charles Inc
The series is distributed in Australia by Wren Publishing Pty Ltd, Melbourne

THE HOLY ISLAND OF LINDISFARNE AND THE FARNE ISLANDS

by R. A. and D. B. Cartwright

DAVID & CHARLES

NEWTON ABBOT   LONDON   NORTH POMFRET (VT)   VANCOUVER

ISBN 0 7153 7185 1
Library of Congress Catalog Card Number 76–2888

Set in 11 on 13pt Baskerville
and printed in Great Britain
by Latimer Trend & Company Ltd Plymouth
for David & Charles (Publishers) Limited
Brunel House Newton Abbot Devon

Published in the United States of America
by David & Charles Inc
North Pomfret Vermont 05053 USA

Published in Canada
by Douglas David & Charles Limited
1875 Welch Street North Vancouver BC

To Our Parents

CONTENTS

ILLUSTRATIONS

(Photographs and drawings by the authors unless otherwise
acknowledged)

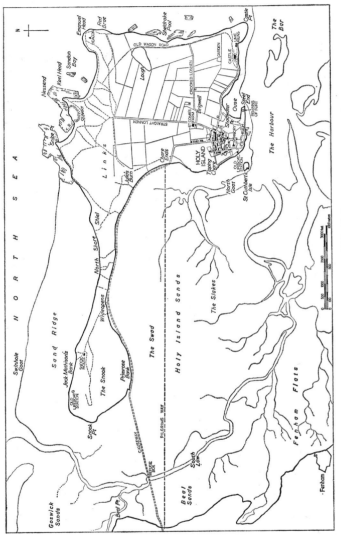

The Holy Island of Lindisfarne

PREFACE

THERE are three Holy Islands in the British Isles, each so called through their early connections with Christianity. Of these three the English Holy Isle of Lindisfarne is perhaps the best known, being the most important historically, the most picturesque and the most accessible. This happy combination of features has given Holy Island, the holiest place in Britain, its wide reputation; unfortunately these factors have also led to many of its present-day problems.

Holy Island has had two other names in the past. Its Celtic name was *Metcaud* or *Metgoit*, but its use gradually disappeared when the English invaders destroyed the Romano-British resistance in the north. The English or Saxon name was *Lindisfaronaea* or *Lindisfarne*. Symeon of Durham says the island took its name from a stream whose mouth was opposite the island, but as no large stream exists or is elsewhere recorded, it is possible that this is a mistake for the channel or gut to the west of the island, known as the Low. It is the Low that separates it from the mainland and which has to be forded to get to the island. It has also been suggested that the stream was a ditch which drains into the Low, but this is of recent origin. A further theory is that the inhabitants of the island came from Lindsey in Lincolnshire. Other than the similarity of the name, there is no evidence for this; as the element *Lind-on* is Old English for water and *Farona* means island, the name could refer to those who pass over the sea to the island. The Norman name, *Insula Sacra*, the Holy Island, has been widely used in official papers and manuscripts since the eleventh century.

The unique feature of the Holy Island of Lindisfarne is the tide and it is not surprising that one of the earliest reports of the island makes a note of this point: 'Which place, as the tide flows and ebbs twice a day, is enclosed by the waves of the sea like an island; and again, twice in a day, when the shore is left dry, becomes contiguous to the land'.

1   GEOGRAPHY AND GEOLOGY

HOLY ISLAND lies about a mile off the Northumberland coast near Beal, some eight miles south of
Berwick-upon-Tweed. When seen from the A1 north
of Belford on a calm, cloudless day at high tide, the isle is a
magnificent sight, mirrored in the blue sea and dominated by
the castle on its tall rock. Seen from Fenham Mill on the coast,
the isle appears much lower; the village becomes more prominent, with the water tower and priory ruins enclosing the houses.
As one approaches the present-day causeway the island appears
to go flatter and more featureless.

The metalled causeway at Beal is now the only safe way to
cross to the island. The tide covers the sands twice a day and
also submerges the causeway. Before this was built there were
several possible tracks; one of these, known as the Pilgrims'
Way, ran east from the Beal road end straight across the Low,
just south of the present-day bridge, to the road at Chare Ends
on the island. A series of nineteenth-century wooden posts and
much older piles of stones mark the route. Two refuge boxes
were built along this way and a cart track ran just to the north
of the poles. In addition to crossing the Low, this route had to
cross a channel of the North Goat at Shelly Bat. A second route,
which was always the safest, is now followed by the road. This
was marked by poles to Primrose Bank on the Snook and by
more poles at the Wideopens along the neck of the Snook. A
third track came from the north and was marked by posts from
Goswick across Goswick sands to join the preceding track half
a mile west of the Snook.

The southern channels of the Low have deepened over the last century and the North Goat has shifted in position, for other routes across the sands marked by early map-makers are now impossible to follow. One from Fenham village crossed the Black Low and South Low to join the Pilgrims' Way across the Swad; it then left this route half a mile west of Chare Ends and headed direct for Tripping Chare. A still earlier route went direct from Fenham Mill to Tripping Chare.

On foot, without tide tables and a clear knowledge of the route, crossing to the island was indeed hazardous. Nowadays in a vehicle there is a tendency to think no danger exists, despite the numerous warnings for caution and the prominent display of tide tables.

ISLAND SCENERY

The island is an axe-shaped plot of land with about 2 square miles above the high water mark. The entire north side, from Snook Point in the west to Emanuel Head in the east, is covered by sand dunes 3 miles in length and between 200 yd and ½ mile wide. The narrowest point is at the neck of the Snook. The Snook is the shaft of the axe and the first part of the island to be encountered. It is surrounded on three sides by a network of channels which can be seen at low tide. The major ones are the Swinhoe Goat to the north which connects the Low to the west and south. An offshoot of the Swinhoe Goat once existed directly west of Snook Point and was called Bloody Bay. The Snook itself is a confused array of sand dunes, some reaching a height of 40ft. This area was once used as a military range. The track leaving the metalled road past Primrose Bank leads to an isolated house which was built in association with the ranges. These have vanished, but Snook House is still inhabited. Nearby is a tower marking an old coal boring. There is an old lime kiln towards Jack Mathison's Bank and, farther west, a disused life-boat station.

A rocky outcrop on the north side of the Snook includes an

old limestone quarry. The Snook was a valuable rabbit warren and salmon netters used to work off its north coast, the stumps of wood which held their nets having only recently disappeared. The majority of dunes are now controlled by the Nature Conservancy Council, with the exception of an area around Snook House and, at the moment, part of the neck of the Snook east of Shell Road and west of the Shiel which is in use as a council rubbish dump.

The dunes to the north of the major part of the island are known as the Links, a small area of which was once a nine-hole golf course. Before that time, the south-western part of the Links was the site of the Kennedy Lime Works. In its heyday this had a complex of a dozen lime kilns, workmen's cottages, a smithy and a couple of wells plus several miles of wagonway. Two tracks went to quarries at Snipe Point and Nessend, while a third branched towards Seal Gut, an easterly extension of Swinhoe Goat (or Gut). The fourth wagonway—the site of which is the only part of this complex that can still easily be seen—ran south from the Southerly Well and its small stream known as Julia's Burn. This is now rough land west of the agricultural land between Julia's Burn and Chare Ends. This wagonway once left the island near Tripping Chare and extended into the North Goat by means of a jetty. The Links dunes are higher than those on the Snook, the highest being 6oft above sea level and used occasionally as a coastguard lookout point. At the east end of the dunes the course of another, later wagonway can be traced; it ran from a quarry at Nessend along the east coast to the disused lime kilns near the castle.

To the north of the island proper are two massive outcrops of rocks which are normally covered at high tide; those to the west under Snipe Point are called Black Skerrs and those to the east Castle Head Rocks. Between them is the Coves Bay, whilst to the east lies Sandon Bay—a beautiful half moon of sand with a central small outcrop of rocks called Keel Head. The east end of Sandon Bay is marked by Emanuel Head with its white navigational beacon just to the north of its highest point.

The centre of the island is flat agricultural land. The landscape is unbroken even by large trees, the few that survive having been stunted and deformed by the wind and drowned by flood water. This area is divided by two major tracks: the Straight and Crooked Lonnen or Lanes. There are a few barns and houses outside the village, and one farm. The remains of another farm may be seen to the south of the Lough, an area of seasonal water to the north and east of the farm land. The Lough is connected to the Ouse by a long drainage ditch. Although there are a few walls, most field boundaries are hedges. The field pattern is largely the result of the late eighteenth-century enclosures.

The east and west coasts are both slightly higher than the centre of the island, and the north is higher than the south by a few feet, so all the farm land tends to drain into the Ouse. The west coast is similar in character to the Snook north of Chare Ends, while the east coast, which faces the roughest seas, is rocky with a shingly beach and low exposed banks of soil above the high-water mark, like the south-west coast.

The south of the island has a series of rocky outcrops, the two largest being the Heugh in the west overlooking the village and, in the east, Beblowe Crag on which the castle sits dramatically. Towards Castle Point are the impressive remains of lime kilns and in between there are ruins probably belonging partly to the castle and partly to the lime-kiln waste dumps. Just to the north of the castle is a wet area once known as the Stank. Near the Riding Stone to the west of the castle are the remains of a wooden jetty built to ship the lime from the kilns near Castle Point. The only common land in the south flanks the Ouse and is bordered by stone walls. Here boats may be beached and there are huts that contain most of the fishing gear used on the island; some of them are made from the upturned hulks of old fishing boats. The west end of the Ouse is marked by the Heugh.

This wedge of dolerite is over 6oft high and extends into the Ouse at Steel End. On the Heugh is the coastguard station, the war memorial, a flagstaff, navigational posts, a cockpit, the remains of a seventeenth-century blockhouse and a ruined building marked on the early Ordnance Survey maps as a chapel. The chapel, cockpit and other parts of the Heugh have never been excavated and so remain rather mysterious. To the west the Heugh overshadows the outer courtyard of the Priory and the adjoining Mustard Close. A few fishermen's huts are located to the south of the Heugh where, until recently, was the life-boat station.

The village

The 'town' of Holy Island is approached from the mainland by Chare Ends road, flanked to the east by a row of twentieth-century bungalows and houses. The town contains many gems of Northumbrian domestic architecture: single-storeyed houses with pantiled roofs and small-paned windows, interspersed with two-storeyed buildings and high old walls. Most streets are narrow, except for the Market Square and Fiddler's Green. Houses are found in unexpected places and conform to no readily discernable plan. Many have been pulled down near Priory Lane and Fiddler's Green, while the older ones are being renovated, especially those owned by mainlanders, as second homes or places for retirement. The old herring houses near the Ouse, for example, are now much improved in appearance. There are also a few new houses by the vicarage and on Palace Hill. At the northern end of the village, which is overshadowed by the water tower near Lewins Lane, the houses were built during the prosperous nineteenth century, when many others were modernised. The only building which ill fits the town, besides the water tower, is the Lindisfarne Mead Factory.

The entire village was designed to accommodate several hundred people. Its present depopulation gives the place an empty look and rather a tranquil air. The medieval village,

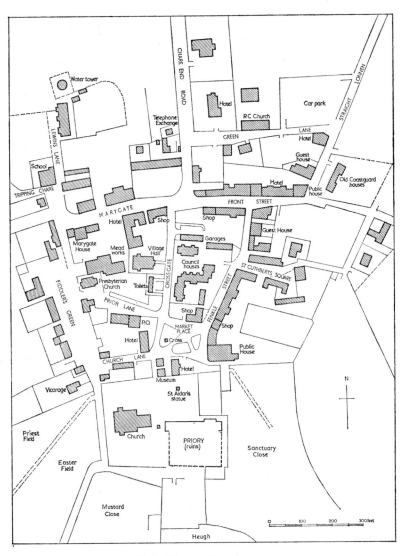

Holy Island village in 1974

with its small cottages, mansions and walled gardens, can still be picked out. The antiquity of the island is reflected in the place names, many of them still in use: Beblowe (Bible Law), Mustard (Minster) Close, Sanctuary (Cemetery) Close, Bigg (Barley) Close, Polly (Palace) Hill, Baggot (Backgate), Cuddy (St Cuthbert's) Walls, Marygate, Crossgate, Piet Hill and Popple Well. Other names recall long-dead islanders: Jenny Bell's Well, Lilburn's Cottage, Lewin's Lane, Willy Potts' Rock and Jack Mathison's Bank. Some are entirely descriptive: Fiddler's Green, Tripping Chare, Primrose Bank, Fenkle (Crooked) Street.

FORMATION OF THE ISLAND

The features of the Northumberland coast began to develop as the North Sea was formed some 8–10,000 years ago, separating Britain from the continent of Europe. The rocks of the island date from Carboniferous times, when those exposed to the north and east were formed and the hard dolerite of the southern part of the island was produced.

There are seven strata of rock on Holy Island, all formed in the middle Carboniferous and laid down in sequence. However, slight earth movements since then have caused the rocks along the north coast to dip to the south-east, while those exposed along the east and south coasts dip to the east. The exposed rocks from each strata have been gradually worn away by the elements, so that the oldest strata are found to the north and west, and those formed slightly more recently to the south and east. The rocks disappear under the dunes and the agricultural land, and are probably deficient under parts of the central land mass of the island.

Sequence of rocks

The seven strata, from the youngest to the oldest, are: the sandstone along the east coast; the Sandbanks limestone at

Geomorphology of Holy Island

COASTAL DEPOSITS

Sand
Gravel
Pebble Ridge

ROCK OUTCROPS

Limestone
Sandstone
Shale
Dolerite

Dune Ridge (height of crest in feet)
Slacks
Limestone Quarry
Cliffs
D Dune Sand
A Agricultural Land
Drainage Channel

—25— Contours (feet)
△ c Triangulation Stations (feet)
f' Faults
• Spot Heights (feet)
✓⁹ Dip and Strike of Strata

Scale

Metres 0   300   600   900
Feet 0   1000   2000   3000

Keel Head
Emanuel Head
Cowes Haven
Quarry
Sand Ridge
Southern Limit of Dunes
Trees Inclined
Chare Ends
Village
Lough Head
Sheldrake Pool
Castle Point
Castle
The Ouse
Steel End
tower
Causeway

Castle Head, Keel Head and to the south of the castle; the sandstone of the north-shore cliffs west of Castle Head Rock; the shale with ironstone nodules from the coves and the south-west of the village; the Acre limestone from the north shore to the south of Snipe Point and to the south of the Heugh; some shales which are not well exposed except by bore holes, and the Eelwell limestone to the north of Snook Tower.

The oldest of the limestones, the Eelwell, is only exposed at low water. Various coal strata are often associated with the limestones and a boring at the Snook has demonstrated this:

Strata	Width	Depth
Sand	6ft	6ft
Clay	7ft	13ft
Eelwell Limestone	3ft	16ft
Coal	6in	16ft 6in
Various other layers		
Coal	6in	143ft
Various other layers		
Coal	1ft	170ft 4in

This coal was commercially worked for brief periods in the eighteenth century. Borings at other parts of the island have also revealed coal. At the Shiel, for example, where the Snook joins the main part of the island, 6–8in of coal underlie 2ft of limestone at 14ft, with a further layer of coal 1–1½ft thick lower down. This is probably the Shilbottle coal.

The Acre limestone was quarried from Snipe Point, 40yd to the north of which, out to sea, the coal strata are exposed. This gradually breaks up and provides sea coal in reasonable amounts on the sandy beaches of the island. The strata over-lying the Acre limestone contains ironstone nodules, which Nathaniel Winch claimed in 1817 to have once been collected from the north shore and used by the Carron Iron Company in their Firth of Forth furnaces. These shales are in turn under a thick bed of soft pale yellow sandstone which can be seen hollowed out into caves at the base of the north shore cliffs. The uppermost of the three limestone layers may be seen at Nessend and also forms the skeirs of Castle Head and Keel Head rocks. This Sandbanks limestone was quarried by the Lower Kennedy Mine and the later Dundee Company; consequently the natural shape of the headland has been considerably altered. The limestone has also been demonstrated by boring just to the north of Straight Lonnen, where it was 9ft deep under clay, but a boring 100yd south on the east side of the lane showed only sand.

All the Carboniferous strata have fossils, but the largest recorded from the island—a 6ft specimen of *Actinoceras giganteum*—was found in the Sandbanks limestone. In the south, Acre limestone is seen under the Heugh and the overlying shale is also exposed south of the Heugh and west of the village. The ironstone nodules it contains are 3–9in in diameter and disc shaped, aligned along the bedding plane of the shale. The uppermost strata form a rock shelf along the east coast and consist of red and grey sandstones with, to the north, beds of dark fireclay shales and coaly layers. These beds just underlie the Great Dryburn Limestone found on the mainland but not on the island.

The dyke

The most notable and spectacular features of relief on the island are produced by a dolorite dyke. A geological dyke is formed by molten rock cooling in a vertical position underground and becomes exposed as the surrounding softer rock wears away. The texture and composition of the dyke is similar to the Whin Sill found farther south; probably both were formed at the same time. The dyke has altered the sedimentary rock it traverses, as may be seen on the south side of the Heugh —the shale is baked and bleached, while limestone is white and crystalline and at some points caught up in the basalt.

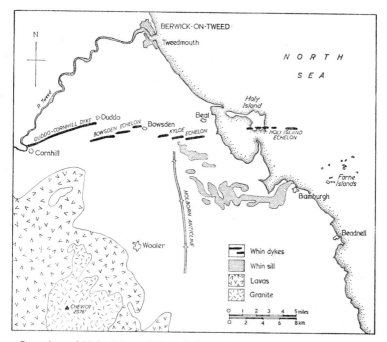

Location of Holy Island dyke echelon, the Whin Sill and the Farne Islands

The Holy Island dyke consists of an echelon in seven parts, the entire series running nearly due east. The most westerly part is Hob Thrush under St Cuthbert's Island; next comes the Heugh, which rises to a height of 62ft and is 50–60yd long. A low dyke marks the east end of the Ouse between the Riding Stone and the Cockle Stone, whilst Beblowe rises to 100ft and is 70yd long. East of Beblowe there is Scar Jockey on the foreshore; then the Plough rock, half a mile off shore, and the Goldstone, 2 miles out to sea, both with dangerous associated reefs. Originally it was thought that the various breaks in the dyke were due to earth movements after it had been formed; thus the Ouse would have been the result of a break between the Cockle Stone segment and the Heugh. A recent and de-

23

tailed examination of the way the molten rock formed the dyke suggests that there has been no movement and that the molten rock tracked to its present site and solidified just there. In addition the dolerite is so hard that very little alteration in the shape of the dykes has taken place since formation.

Glacial deposits

Upon the basic rock structure of the island, the ice ages have imposed various deposits which include boulder clays and boulders, gravels and sands. A good section of clays may be seen on the cliff near Tripping Chare. The clays rest on sandy shale and sandstone. At one point the drag of the glacier which deposited the clay can be seen to produce a lens-shaped buckled effect in the underlying sandstone. There is other evidence of glacial action at Red Brae, a cliff on the east coast just south of Emanuel Head, where an immense discoid erratic boulder may be seen, together with some coal deposits adhering to the underside. It is embedded in the lowest clay stratum and is at least 62yd long. Boulder clays may be found under the village and in the south-east of the island for ¾ mile to the north of the castle, and along the east coast to Emanuel Head.

During and since glacial times the familiar features of the island have been formed and the exposed strata of rocks worn away to their present form. It is these rocks which are responsible for glacial debris being deposited in the area and forming an island. When the North Sea first formed, the area which became Holy Island consisted of several rocky islets with boulder clay on them, each surrounded by a beach. One islet included the Beblowe area, another the Heugh and village area; and there were others on the Snook and to the north of the modern island. As the sea levels changed, the beaches around these small islands expanded and joined the islets together. These raised beaches may be found on the Snook, along the east coast, and in the centre of the island north of the Ouse.

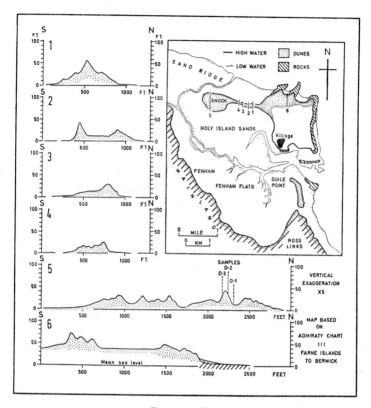

Dune profiles

Beaches and dunes

The stones of these beaches range from the pebble spit at Castle Point and the ridge north-west of the Snook to the gravels of the east and south-west coasts and the sand of the dune systems. The finest rock particles are in the mud and silt around the coasts and also in the alluvial deposits on the island itself. The dunes comprise fine blown sand and, to the south of the Snook, include about 3 per cent shell fragments. The dunes probably extended to the main part of the island at one time, as the same type of sand, with its fine and medium quartz fragments and shells, is also found under the soil in the centre to the south and west of the Lough. The sand dunes are remarkably symmetrical in profile, being slightly steeper to the north. Most dune ridges run east-west. The highest dune in 1970 was 78.3ft above sea level, whilst many dune ridges are over 50ft high. Normally sand dunes are gradually colonised by plants which fix the sand and enable larger and larger plants to grow, until finally trees are established. This final phase has not been reached on the island, although there are a few shrubs in one corner of the dunes. Dune slacks—marshy areas which seasonally form pools—can be found between the ridges in the more stable parts.

Pools and soils

The other surface water on Holy Island is also largely seasonal nowadays and consists of pools by the castle, to the south of Crooked Lonnen and the Lough. The Lough has started to dry out in recent years, especially in summer, while other pools to the south of the agricultural land more frequently hold water. Judging by the alluvial deposits at the centre of the island the Ouse and Lough were continuous at one time.

The soils, which have yet to be fully investigated, seem to be similar to those on the nearby mainland, based on sand and alluvium. One part of the island, near Tripping Chare, is especially interesting. Here the metre-thick, very dark soil horizon must have accumulated by some special process, perhaps intensive cultivation or as the result of kelp burning.

Holy Island is surrounded by a complicated series of sand banks, salt marshes, mud flats and silty deposits with many indispersed salt-water channels known as guts or goats. Salt marshes tend to increase in area, but every so often high tides and winds wash away parts of them. For similar reasons the channels through the mud and sand change from time to time. The sands are found largely to the north of the island on the

spit known as Goswick Sand Rig and also just to the south of
the Snook. The mud and silt are largely to the east of the Low
near the mainland, an area known as Fenham Flats. Much of
this area is being colonised by *Spartina* grass and salt marsh, as
is a strip to the south of the Snook.

The basic geology of the island is fairly simple but the post-
glacial events that have produced the island of today are
imperfectly known. The sand dunes may hide any amount of
interesting archaeological material, for all that is known of their
development and changes over the years.

Many small-scale maps of England and Northumberland include Holy Island, but with little useful detail. The few large-
scale maps which exist are a useful adjunct to documentary
sources, while some give information about the island not found
elsewhere. Unfortunately, before the Ordnance Survey, map-
ping conventions and surveying techniques varied a great deal.
The outline of an island, for example, could show high, low or
intermediate water levels.

The earliest detailed map, first published in 1610 and re-
printed many times, is that of John Speed, who shows an island
little different from today, except around the Ouse. There is a
broad stream entering the Ouse from the west, apparently
draining the Lough, which Speed calls Shelrak Pool. The castle
appears to consist of several buildings rather than the present
single unit, and the track linking the village and the castle
crossed the Lough stream by the King's Bridge. There are two
other unique features: a cross marked just to the south of the
Coves and a gibbet on the Snook. From the accompanying
description, Speed suggests that the castle and a blockhouse
just to the south-east both defended the harbour. Other
seventeenth-century maps include the work of John Blaeu,
published some time after 1645 and taken in part from Speed.

There are small differences in the shape of the island and the way geographical features are presented.

The navigational maps of Grenville Collins were first published in 1693. Set with 'south' at the top of the page, they give little island detail, except for the first accurate view of the sands at low water. Wide channels only extend a small distance from the harbour to the west, and the North Goat does not exist; while the South Low is shown only as a trickle extending north past Goswick. Soundings are given in the harbour and out to sea; the 1½ fathoms at the harbour bar are little different from today. Robert Morden's small maps, which appeared from 1695 onwards, are a composite of those by Collins and Speed. They include Collins' mistakes—for example, Hob Thrush is recorded as 'Trush' and Coves Cross and Shelrak Pool are corrupted to 'Cover Cross' and 'Sharak Pool'.

More interesting and accurate is the map of a military survey of 1673. This shows no outside influences and was never printed. It comprises a plan of the island to the scale of 1in: 300yd and gives soundings taken in the harbour and out to sea, as well as details of the village. Entitled *The Ground Plott of Holy Island upon the coaste of Northumberland near Berwick. Survey in the yeare one thousand sixe seventy three*, the document includes three scale plans: two of the 'Olde Castle' and one of the 'Plattforme and Redoutte made and designed by Dan. Collingwood Esquire and Mr Rbt Trollopp'. This is the fort at Steel End, which is often quoted as being built in 1675. However, there is another date, 1683, on the document, near the plans of the fort; so the map could have been drawn then, the survey having taken place earlier. The plan shows how the castle appeared at the time, as well as the considerable size of the fort at Steel End, which was about the same overall length as the castle. All that may be seen today is the 'redoutte'.

A contemporary schematic drawing of a view of the south of the island shows the Heugh, Hob Thrush, the Priory, Steel End and the castle. The vertical perspective is ignored, but the ruins

28

of the Priory are shown clearly and are much more complete than they appear even in eighteenth-century drawings. The 1673 map is remarkable for what it shows of seventeenth-century Holy Island. Except for a small area around the village, it was unenclosed and featureless. The village, small and compact, consisted of a few detached houses and rows of smaller cottages, together with small areas of land enclosed by walls or hedges—the messuages and garths of medieval documents. The Lough is large, drained by a stream which runs a tortuous course, firstly towards a point at the centre of the Heugh and then running round the base of the Heugh to enter the Ouse from the west. The channel is wide and crossed by a bridge near the present site of the Brigwell in Crooked Lonnen. As the stream nears the Ouse, there are several large channels by the Ouse in the place now known as Shadwater. The Ouse had dried up slightly since mapped by Speed earlier in the century.

Another documentary plan, produced about 1724, to the scale 8in:1 mile, shows a largely unenclosed island, with the remains of a medieval village pattern and a few small fields between the present-day Sanctuary Close and Chare Ends. The village plan is similar to the 1673 map except for a few minor changes. The pools just to the north of the Ouse are marked as one large pond the size of the Lough.

In 1769 an entirely new 1in:1 mile map of Northumberland was published by Andrew Armstrong. This beautiful map gives little detail of the island; it shows the Ouse and Lough rather schematically and very different from the earlier plans. In the village it marks Marygate and part of Fenkle Street and notes some ruins to the east of the castle, possibly some of the outer defences noted by Speed. It is the first map to show the stones across the sands marking the Pilgrims' Way, as well as another route to the island by Fenham and Tripping Chare. On the next important printed map—Fryer's of 1820—the channel of the South Low cuts this route, making it impossible to cross direct from Fenham.

Several large-scale plans were made of the island and village in 1792 and 1793 by Thomas Wilkin and his pupils in association with the enclosing of the island. There were two enclosure schemes put forward; the second after the first one had been disputed. Some maps show both divisions and others just the second one which was implemented. About half the island was enclosed by hedges or walls and the resultant field pattern remains to this day. By this date the Lough was emptied by a drain and sluice, and the site of the old pools in the fields to the west of the Ouse were named Shadwater even when they had been drained. No farm was marked on the maps and the site of the King's Bridge was noted as Brigwell Lane, now called Crooked Lonnen. The small medieval land patterns around the village disappeared into the larger field patterns, although some of the older field names were retained—Bigg Close, Great Baggot and Sea Sheet, for example. Place names for the rest of the island included Thistley Hill, Castle Foot, The Bents, Sprat Pools and Bible Hill.

The absence of farms is surprising, but by 1819 an estate plan marks as a homestead what is now St Coomb's Farm, although this is not shown on Fryer's map of 1820. However, Greenwood's excellent map of 1827 and 1828 does mark this farm, as well as Lilburn's Cottage and the 'Lough House', the farm just south-east of the Lough. This is named 'Lough Farm' in the first edition Ordnance Survey of 1859; St Coomb's Farm is also present but not named. An estate plan of about 1880 marks a field to the *west* of Chare Ends Road as 'St Coombs' and notes that there are four farms on the island: Lough, Town and two unnamed ones. The Town Farm is the St Coomb's Farm of today, though it is not named 'St Coomb's' on a map until 1920. It seems that the farm was not the site of a medieval chapel, which if it ever existed, would more probably be to the west of Chare Ends in what is now farm land. The fields to the west of the Chare Ends Lane included two medieval lanes, known as Butt Chair and Berwick Chair, which disappeared after the enclosure. The farm by the Lough ceased to exist sometime before 1920.

Since 1859 the various editions of the Ordnance Survey have recorded the disappearance of some of the old buildings and the emergence of new houses and bungalows. The older place names have gradually changed; what was once Thistley Hill Road is now Crooked Lonnen, and Quarry Road has become the Straight Lonnen. Since 1963 the island has been mapped by students and staff from Newcastle University so that changes on a year-to-year basis may be studied.

The study of maps gives some idea of the island in medieval times. The village may have been founded very early after the Norman settlement in the north as a planned town, based on a broad green with small parcels of land sold for house development. This could correspond to the time when the priory was first built as a cult church to St Cuthbert. The wars with Scotland upset these plans and only a few clues are left to this early attempt at town planning. For example, the village is known as the 'town' and the word 'chare' is used for city lanes not villages. The early maps show the north side of Marygate, the west side of Fiddler's Green and the east side of Fenkle Street to have formed the three sides of a very large green, long since built on; the only grassy parts remaining are Fiddler's Green and the Market Square. Supporting the town idea is the fact that the island was a designated medieval borough. The names of the medieval fields have survived in the Barley Field (Bigg Close) and several fields to the north of the village, known as 'sheets'. This may be a version of the term 'sheth', a strip; perhaps the remnant of the medieval strip system on Holy Island. The rest of the medieval island was probably not enclosed and was doubtless used for grazing and rabbit rearing.

WATER SUPPLY

Although there is plenty of seasonal standing water in the dunes and on the agricultural land, it has never been used for regular consumption. George Johnston records in 1854 that a shower of rain on the island was marked by much local activity to collect the downpour in tubs and buckets. Since earliest times the islanders have relied on a series of relatively shallow wells. The water collects in the rock strata, so that borings have to be made near to the coast, and this often meant that the water became polluted with salt after a high tide, as happened to Jenny Bell's Well. The most reliable was Popple Well, near the store of rocket apparatus, and others may be seen close to Tripping Chare, in the priory and by the monastery cottages opposite the Iron Rails.

The present water supply comes from a bore hole near Lewins Lane. The site was first bored in 1951, when the first 50ft were of soil, sand and clay, followed by two bands of limestone, shales and sandstone. At 132ft there was a grey shale layer with ironstone nodules which is the end of the bore. This well produces a good supply, but the ironstone tends to disintegrate and produce a red sediment which can cloud the water unless the tank is washed regularly. The supply is very similar chemically to the water from Popple Well, except that the bore has slightly more nitrogenous elements, fewer iron salts in solution and is somewhat less clear.

CLIMATE

The Northumbrian coastal area has a relatively mild maritime climate, with an average rainfall of 23.29in in the year. The average temperature in July is 14.5°C and in January 3.4°C. These temperatures reflect the typical cool summers and mild winters of Holy Island. In general the climate on Lindisfarne and along the north-east coast of England resembles that of the south-east corner of Scotland, and these records are taken from Berwick-on-Tweed, since no separate meteorological recordings have been made on Holy Island.

Typical features of the local climate are the constant breeziness, the clear bracing air, the chilly spring weather and raw north-easterly winds. Westerly gales are most likely in October, December and January, while northerlies prevail in late winter and early spring. Snow falls on an average of eighteen days in the year, and ground frost and morning fog are more common in the northern part of Northumberland than in the south of the county.

NATURAL HISTORY

BIRD LIFE

THE bird populations seen around Holy Island are re-markable both in terms of the wide variety of species recorded and, in certain cases, the sheer numbers of them. Richard Perry in 1946 noted 268 species and subspecies on the island or around its shores, including doubtfuls, and a further twenty-three within a ten-mile radius. Since then a further twenty species new to the island have been recorded, making an all-time total of 311 species, 220 of which have been seen in the last five years. The island lies on several migratory routes and, in addition, has sheltered stretches of both fresh and salt water, and over 6,000 acres of sand and mud flats. The channels and flats support a wide variety of specialised feeders. The island is also near the breeding colonies on the Farne Islands and the Isle of May, whose occupants obtain some of their food requirements in the vicinity of Lindisfarne.

The check list (see Appendix C) includes only a relatively small number of breeding and resident birds. Perry noted thirty-four in the 1940s, whilst a more recent list notes forty-four; although it would be pleasant to record that this was due to the establishment of the island's nature reserve, it probably results from the creation of further suitable nesting habitats. There are two notable breeding species: the eider and the fulmar. The main concentration of eiders, breeding in north-eastern England, is to be found on the Farne Islands, but several pairs breed on Lindisfarne and the neighbouring mainland, and many more feed on the shellfish around the island. Local numbers usually exceed 1,000 in winter, with a maximum count of 2,000 in October 1970. The fulmar breeds in two localities on Holy Island, both well documented by Perry. A colony was established at the Coves in 1927 and still supports thirty to forty pairs, whilst another twelve or so pairs are to be found breeding around the castle and lime kilns.

A large variety of sea birds are seen regularly from the island, including gannets, no doubt mainly from the colony on Bass Rock; kittiwakes and guillemots from St Abb's Head and the Farne Islands, as well as puffins, shags and cormorants from the Farne Islands.

It is during the winter months that the greatest numbers of birds are to be seen around Holy Island. At this time the relatively small breeding populations of wildfowl and waders are greatly swelled by the influx of winter visitors breeding in arctic and sub-arctic regions, from Iceland, Greenland and Spitzbergen to Scandinavia and Russia.

Wildfowl

From the wildfowlers' point of view, the ducks are the most important winter visitors. The principal quarry species is the wigeon, flocks of which begin to assemble in late August and build up to a winter peak of between 20,000 and 30,000 by the end of November or December, according to the severity of the continental winter. The next most numerous species prized by wildfowlers is the mallard; its winter flocks have only occasionally exceeded 1,000 in recent years. The other surface-feeding duck, such as pintail, teal and shoveler, are present in smaller numbers.

Apart from the eider, other diving ducks that are numerous in winter are the long-tailed duck and common scoter which may be seen in rafts off the Ross Back Sands. Lindisfarne is second in importance among British estuaries for numbers of ducks, geese and swans, according to *The Birds of Estuaries*

Inquiry Report, 1972-3; higher numbers being recorded only in the Firth of Forth.

The commonest geese are the greylag and Brent. The greylag is a regular winter visitor in increasing numbers; 150 were seen on the nature reserve in 1969, and over 600 were recorded in 1974. Occasional flocks in excess of 1,200 have been observed in the vicinity, making it one of the major sites in England. Inevitably there have been noticeable changes in the bird populations at Lindisfarne since Abel Chapman wrote of his pursuit of Brent geese with gun and punt. In those days several thousand dark-bellied Brent geese, from populations nesting in Arctic Russia and Siberia, appeared during severe winters; and, even in relatively mild ones, some hundreds were recorded. Nowadays birds of the dark-bellied race are few, and the light-bellied Brent from Spitzbergen make this their only regular wintering ground in Britain; while several thousands have occurred, the winter peak has seldom exceeded 700 in recent years.

Following a marked reduction in the world population of Brent geese, after an epidemic destroyed much of the eel grass in the early 1930s, they were given full protection in Britain.

Winter herds of mute swans regularly numbered over 400 before 1968, but now fewer than twenty birds visit the Slakes. Bewick's swans are regularly recorded, but in very small numbers. Whooper swans, however, are abundant, with peak winter numbers exceeding 400 in recent years—larger than at any other English wintering ground.

Waders

Waders, attracted by the richness of the local food supplies, assemble in winter and probe the mud for a variety of worms, shellfish and crustaceans, according to their size, length of bill and precise method of feeding. The most common wader is the dunlin, with flocks up to 20,000 recorded from October to March. The knot is also commonly seen in flocks of 10,000 or so, while another abundant wader, the bar-tailed godwit, appears regularly in winter in flocks of 3,000–7,000. The recorded winter counts for all wader species have varied over recent years between 37,000 and 46,000—remarkable figures by British standards. *The Birds of Estuaries Inquiry Report,* 1972–3, lists the principal estuaries and the numbers of waders seen at each. Lindisfarne, ranking thirteenth in the listed sites, is on a numerical par with such famous wader haunts as the Burry Inlet, the Humber and Strangford Lough.

The common gull is, appropriately, the most abundant of all the gulls, with winter numbers exceeding 10,000, whilst the herring and black-headed gulls are numerous throughout the year, the latter having bred on the Lough since about 1894.

In addition to the winter visitors, many species are recorded on migration. For the birdwatcher on Holy Island a most exciting prospect is presented when adverse weather conditions in autumn bring a fall of warblers, chats and pipits, with the possibility of a red-backed shrike or bluethroat to add variety to the checklist. The full list for the island and its neighbourhood includes a number of species, such as king eider, Pallas's sandgrouse, and rustic bunting, which have been observed only once or twice since detailed records have been kept. Undoubtedly the list will be added to as further chance occurrences bring birds within binocular range of the birdwatcher.

ANIMAL LIFE

Despite its small size and generally bare, windswept appearance, the island supports a wide range of amphibians, reptiles and mammals. The common frog, the common toad, the crested and smooth newts, and the common lizard have all been recorded as breeding residents. Moles, shrews, voles and hedgehogs are also common breeding species. There may be as many as four or five breeding pairs of foxes, whilst rats, stoats and weasels are often found around the farms and fishermen's huts.

37

Many of these species may be supplemented by mainland animals from time to time, and such is clearly the source of the solitary roe deer seen on the Snook each year since 1970. In recent winters, brown hares have visited the island and can often be seen on the Links, but by far the commonest land mammal is the rabbit. The warren on the Snook was an important part of the annual income of the island in medieval times and the islanders often used to take advantage of rabbit as a readily available alternative to fish. The large populations were drastically reduced by myxomatosis and rabbits are unlikely again to increase to their former abundance.

Seals, the most characteristic of the area, are by no means the only marine mammals to be seen from the island. The common porpoise is regularly recorded in summer and packs of killer whales are occasionally seen offshore. Paradoxically the commonest local seal is the grey seal, whilst the common seal is only seen occasionally, although it may have been much commoner in the past—historical accounts often confused the two species. Visitors crossing the causeway bridge may see one or two grey seals in the Low. Nessend rocks are also a favoured site and up to forty of them may be seen here on a calm day. Most originate from the Farnes, although there have been reports of cows calving in Sandon Bay. In the past, islanders have occasionally hunted seals, driving groups into shallow water and slaughtering them, as is recalled by Bloody Bay, the name of a blind channel which once existed to the west of the Snook.

INSECTS

Insects recorded from the island range in size from the gigantic fly, *Larvaerora grossa*, to primitive winged insects such as the thrips. The vast majority of recent records are for common and widely distributed insects, but two heteropterans are noteworthy: *Macrotylus paykulli*, here at its most northerly point of distribution, and *Heterogaster artemisiae*, another rare creature normally found locally in the south of England.

Because the butterfly and moth populations are some way from those on the mainland, it was thought that new variants might be found on the island. Two butterflies in which such variations occur are the dark green fritillary and the grayling, but all specimens so far examined appear to be similar to those from the mainland colonies. In these species, at least, the isolation of the island has not apparently resulted in the separation of its populations from those of the mainland. The small elephant hawk moth, the sand dart and the Chinese character are typically coast and dune species, but Holy Island is the northern limit of their distribution. The other recorded *Lepidoptera* are those which one would expect to find in a coastal locality and are generally distributed throughout the British Isles.

PLANT LIFE

Holy Island and its environs support a varied and interesting flora. A recent check list (see Appendix B) notes 418 flowering plants, including a number of rare or unusual species. Not surprisingly, the Lough and the agricultural land have very different plant populations from those found on sand, shingle and mud. The salt marsh has its characteristic plants as have the northern cliffs and the southern whin dyke. The sand dunes are particularly important because these and their associated 'slacks' are the last unspoilt dunes of Northumberland and much of the typical dune flora is still present.

The island's nature reserve includes a range of plant communities showing the colonisation of bare sandy shores through embryo dunes to stable dunes and dune grassland. The principal dune-forming species is marram grass, which is dominant over much of Holy Island, though the large, blue-green leaved, sea lyme grass and the sea couch grass contribute to the fixing of the sand at the earliest stage. On the stable dunes, two related species, viper's bugloss and houndstongue, are the most conspicuous plants, the former having blue or red flowers and the latter purple. The dune flora includes some unusual plants, such as the pirri-pirri bur, a plant native to Australia and New Zealand, which became established about sixty years ago. The beautiful grass of parnassus is locally common on damp dune grassland and the large-flowered evening primrose may also be found. Among other dune plants are several species of gentian and centaury, and a grand total of eleven members of the orchid family, including some that are exceedingly rare, although in the damp calcareous hollows between the dunes, dense colonies of northern marsh and meadow orchids may be easily found.

The salt marshes are almost all dominated by cord grass, a relatively recently introduced species which has the remarkable ability to bind unstable mud and silt. On the south side of the island a more varied community occurs with scurvy grass, thrift, sea aster and sea manna grass, forming a complex mosaic with cord grass and sea clubrush. The salt marshes are being carefully watched to see how they increase in size now they are colonised by cord grass. Another feature of the inter-tidal zones are the eel grasses, which are an important item of diet for wigeon, whooper swan and Brent geese, and so have a significant role in the ecology of the entire area. Other typical coastal plants include sea rocket and sea sandwort. The island is also the extreme northern limit of distribution of the sea purslane and the most southerly station of the lovage.

The natural end point of the plant succession commencing with sand dunes is woodland of birch and oak, but this has not developed on the island, though the dune grasslands are being invaded by birch, willow and pine. There are few trees on the agricultural land and most seem to have been planted. Some were established around the Lough over a hundred years ago, but have long since become moribund. Sheltered by the village, sycamores and some horse chestnuts flourish, and there are a few wind-deformed hawthorn and elder bushes.

For the careful observer, the many Holy Island habitats have great rewards to offer. Several hundred different plants await the discerning visitor; many are now rare on the island and several are known to have vanished during the last century. Among these is the oyster plant, a rare species of shingle beaches and highly specialised for its austere habitat, which was originally noted by Dr Johnston. If the dunes become eroded, many plants may be lost—some scarce in Northumberland, others rare anywhere in the country. Thus considerable care should be taken when visiting the dunes and dune slacks, and no plant should ever be picked. Providing visitors take nothing but photographs, the wildlife of the island will remain undamaged for future generations to enjoy. This is the objective of the Nature Conservancy Council in managing the natural parts of the island as a nature reserve.

THE LINDISFARNE NATIONAL NATURE RESERVE

It was the strong local interest in wildfowling that was largely responsible for the establishment of the Lindisfarne National Nature Reserve. With growing affluence, improving communications and increasing car ownership, the number of wildfowlers looking towards Fenham Flats and Holy Island Sands gradually reached a point at which the members of the Northumberland and Durham Wildfowlers' Association felt that the sport was gravely threatened by uncontrolled and indiscriminate shooting, and sought means to alleviate the problem. The Natural History Society of Northumberland, Durham and Newcastle upon Tyne were also concerned about the situation at an early stage because of the threat to local wildfowl.

Following consultations with the national wildfowling organisation—the Wildfowlers' Association of Great Britain and Ireland (WAGBI)—it was suggested to the Nature Conservancy in August 1960 that a wildfowl refuge should be established in the area. After detailed consideration by the Nature Conservancy's Wildfowl Conservation Committee and discussions with the local wildfowlers and naturalists, it was agreed that the Conservancy itself should attempt to create a refuge by securing the shooting rights over a tract of land stretching from Cheswick Black Rocks to Budle Bay, in which the northern and southern areas would be maintained as sanctuaries, while controlled shooting would be permitted in the central part of the area.

The Lindisfarne Wildfowl Panel held its first meeting in August 1963, by which time good progress with land acquisition had been achieved. This body was made up of representatives of the WAGBI, the Northumberland and Durham Wildfowlers' Association and the Natural History Society of Northumberland, Durham and Newcastle upon Tyne (now the Natural History Society of Northumbria). It is charged with advising the Nature Conservancy Council on wildfowling and wildfowl conservation matters and was responsible for devising the system of controlled wildfowling by permit. The panel was joined later by the larger Reserve Joint Advisory Committee, with more diverse representation, which had as one of its first tasks the drafting of bye-laws to protect the wildlife of the reserve.

The first part of the reserve to be acquired was declared on 15 September 1964. This comprised the Snook sand dunes, and the sand and mud flats between high and low water marks north of a line from Longbrig End to Snook Point, and also Chesterhill Slakes and Budle Point in Budle Bay—some 1,665 acres in all. The owners of the intervening coastline, and of a separate coastal strip at Cheswick Black Rocks, subsequently agreed to the inclusion of these areas in the reserve, which at present extends to 8,100 acres.

Each season since the winter of 1965 several hundred permits have been issued by the wildfowl panel, authorising the holders to shoot wildfowl and waders of particular species within the permitted area of Fenham Flats and Holy Island Sands. Goswick Sands, Ross Back Sands and Budle Bay have been maintained as sanctuaries in which birds may feed and roost undisturbed. The activities of the wildfowlers are watched over by the reserve wardens, who also record the number and movements of the wildfowl. A condition of the issue of permits is that each recipient records the dates of visits to the reserve and the number of each species of bird shot. The returns thus provide an index of the shooting pressure which, when related to the numbers of the quarry species, indicate whether any changes in the permit issue systems are necessary to protect the breeding stocks. Thus the old traditions of wildfowling are continued around Holy Island in a fashion acceptable to both fowlers and conservationists.

The aims of the reserve

The principal objectives of the Nature Conservancy Council in managing the reserve are to safeguard the wildfowl and wader populations which overwinter in the area or pass through it on migration, and to allow the controlled exploitation of this resource by wildfowlers. The first of these two aims is an international obligation involving the co-operation of the governments of all the coastal nations of Europe through which the birds migrate, as well as those of sub-arctic and arctic countries where they breed.

An important subsidiary objective is the maintenance in undamaged condition of the plant and animal communities of sand dunes, saltmarsh and mudflat in order to safeguard the species of which they are composed. Examples of natural or near-natural habitats are of considerable value for scientific research. Indeed the reserve can only be effectively managed if its ecology is properly understood, and this understanding is dependant on the results of thorough investigations of the interrelationships of its flora and fauna. The reserve is also of importance as a teaching ground where large numbers of students receive instruction in the elements of ecology; though

43

such use of the area must be carefully controlled to prevent deterioration of the habitats.

A great many amateur naturalists make regular visits to the reserve to study particular groups of animals and plants; it is partly to meet their needs, as well as those of visitors with less specific interests, that the reserve is managed. There is also a moral obligation to look after wildlife as part of the national heritage and a not inconsiderable component of the amenities of the island. Some intervention—in such more or less natural processes as the encroachment of cord grass across the mudflats and birch scrub into areas of dune grassland—is, however, necessary to prevent detrimental changes. Sand dunes are particularly vulnerable to damage and are capable of withstanding only limited recreational pressure; both wind erosion and trampling result in the loss of plant cover. Prompt action is necessary if blowing of the affected dunes is to be prevented; this takes the form of planting the exposed faces with marram grass and cordoning off treated areas to allow the vegetation to recover. Such measures are evident at several sites in the dune systems.

The information services relating to the reserve, though rather limited at present, are to be improved by the setting up of appropriate displays.

HOLY ISLAND'S NATURALISTS

The history of those who have studied the wildlife of the island is as unique as any feature of Lindisfarne, and some of the pioneer natural historians were local men. Dr William Turner, a sixteenth-century naturalist from Morpeth, recorded sea-wormwood from Holy Island, and John Ray, who visited the island in 1671, noted madwort (an introduced species); both of which have long since vanished from the area. Thomas Bewick, the local woodcut artist and naturalist, obtained one or two specimens from Holy Island for his *History of British Birds*.

Several other local naturalists, such as Prideaux Selby, William Hewitson and John and Albany Hancock, stimulated local interest and consolidated the accumulating knowledge on Northumbrian natural history for the mid-nineteenth century. Unfortunately they left no specific details about Holy Island.

The first local field study society in the vicinity of the island was the Berwickshire Naturalists' Club, founded in 1831. The club first met on Holy Island in 1833 and since then has made frequent visits. The Berwickshire naturalists' journal records the first overall account of the island's natural history written by Dr George Johnston in 1854. The early specialists in ornithology were nearly all keen wildfowlers—a very different situation from today. Abel Chapman was one such person, a man of worldwide interests who shot and studied the birds on Holy Island from the 1870s to the 1920s. With a near contemporary, George Bolam, he set the high standard for Holy Island ornithology. Geoffrey Watson, a systematic observer and careful recorder of birds, was on the island for some years in the 1920s and the first fairly complete species list was drawn up by W. B. Alexander in the 1930s. Since then Richard Perry has eclipsed all earlier ornithological work by a careful and detailed account of the island published in 1946. Since the 1940s much more systematic work has been undertaken into all aspects of the island's natural history, largely by scientists from British universities.

3 THE GOLDEN AGE OF LINDISFARNE

MESOLITHIC wanderers of between 8,000 and 2,000 BC visited the island, leaving behind small flint tools of the Tardenois industry, which are now in the Museum of Antiquities in Newcastle upon Tyne. Holy Island provided an ideal locality for these people, who were fond of sandy areas and lived by fishing, fowling and gathering shellfish.

A later Neolithic polished axe head, made of dolerite and measuring 113 × 49 × 24mm, was found in Bishop's Palace Garden in 1926 and donated to the Newcastle Society of Antiquaries. The only other possibly prehistorical find—some 'hearth sites' about 5½ft in diameter, reported to have been discovered on the Snook—could be very much later in origin.

EARLY NORTHUMBRIA

England's north-east coast, probably including Holy Island, was the site of one of the earliest permanent Anglo-Saxon settlements in Britain, Bamburgh being a castle of the kings of Bernicia from AD 547. Saxon Northumbria was formed by the union of the northern kingdom of Bernicia and southern Deira, thereafter Bamburgh became the capital and stronghold of the new kingdom. The earliest Northumbrian documentary sources refer to the time when the Saxons were trying to establish a firm foothold in the area and meeting strong resistance from the

46

local Celtic populations. The most successful was the Celtic leader Urien (Urgben) map Rheged, who originated from near the Solway Firth and fought the Bernician king, Theodric, having made an alliance with other Celtic tribes. Nennius records that '. . . he [Urgben] shut them up for three days and nights in the island of Metcaud [Lindisfarne], and while he was on that expedition he was murdered by Morcant's design out of envy, because in him before all kings there was the greatest courage in carrying on war'.

In this oblique fashion the island is mentioned for the first time, referring to a siege about the year 575, when the place may have been a Saxon military depot and safe harbour. With the murder of Urien, the Celtic efforts to counterattack fell apart and native resistance to the northern Saxons ceased. The Christian Celtic peoples were gradually absorbed by the invaders, especially after their conversion to Christianity. Holy Island was very close to Northumbrian military and civil activities, being near both Bamburgh and Old Yeavering. Despite this, no permanent buildings seem to have been erected on the island.

Edwin (617–33) was the first north Saxon king to be baptised. Celtic sources claim this was performed by a son of Urien, Rhun map Urien, while English sources maintain that Paulinus took charge of the ceremony. It is possible that both stories are correct and refer to different dates. Whatever the truth of the matter, this is a facet of the Celtic-Roman Church controversy which divided the early British Church for many years.

AIDAN

Christianity lapsed briefly after Edwin's death, but was revived as a result of King Oswald's victory, at Deniseburn near Hexham, over his heathen predecessors. Oswald took the Christian faith before the battle and afterwards King Donald of Scotland sent him a monk of Iona to establish the Celtic Church in Northumbria. Carmán made little impression upon the Saxons, being of an 'austere disposition', and soon returned to his island monastery. His reports to the monks of Iona stimulated the interests of one of them, Aidan, who came to Northumbria in 635 or soon afterwards and chose Holy Island as his episcopal see, having been given a choice of anywhere in the kingdom.

There followed a period of intense spiritual, evangelical and intellectual activity unparalleled in the English church and Lindisfarne became the great centre for Christianity in Saxon England for the next 241 years. The fame of the island bishopric spread throughout the western world and pilgrims still visit Lindisfarne in memory of this golden age.

The church Aidan first built on the island was probably, in the Celtic tradition, largely wooden. It did not survive long because the second Bishop of Lindisfarne, Finán (652–61) is said to have rebuilt the church in the Irish manner, using wood and reed thatch. This church was called a cathedral, and Aidan's body was transferred there from the cemetery on the island. The whereabouts of these churches is not known, as excavations have not revealed the site of any pre-Norman buildings, although by tradition the Norman Priory overlies at least one Saxon building. The third bishop, Colmán, was, like Finán, a monk educated on Iona in the traditions of the early Celtic Church. Throughout the episcopy of these early bishops the church on Lindisfarne was becoming more and more attractive to the local Celtic and Saxon nobility as a place of religious learning and contemplation. The attraction was maintained even after the Celtic religious practices were replaced by Roman rules—for example, in 737, King Ceolwulf of Northumbria resigned his throne to become a monk on Holy Island.

THE CELTIC AND ROMAN CHURCHES

Once Christianity was accepted as the state religion by the Roman Empire, the church organisation changed somewhat to

Page 49 (above) Holy Island looking towards the north-west. This aerial photograph was taken before the causeway was built. The physical features of the island are best compared with the general map on page 10; *(below)* causeway bridge and refuge box looking towards the Snook sand dunes; Whooper swans fly overhead

Page 50 Holy Island castle: *(above)* from the south-east, showing the plan of the modern castle, and to the north, the castle garden, soon to be re-opened by the National Trust; *(below)* from the west looking across the Ouse; the remarkable height of Beblowe Crag is shown as well as some modern fishing gear and the islanders' fishing boats

fit the secular administrative system. In consequence, Christianity spread most easily to the provinces of the Old Roman Empire. When the teachings of the church were taken to Ireland by Paladius and Patrick in the fifth century, however, they were confronted by an entirely different social situation—a familial society with many petty kings and a complex system of overlordship. The most important feature of life was a person's position in the social hierarchy; this linked the family unit, the village and the kingdom in a rigid framework. In order to develop, the church had to adapt to this and, instead of becoming the worldly and sophisticated episcopal system of Rome, the opposite came about. The church in Ireland became withdrawn, philosophical and monastic. This proved immensely popular; many Irish noblemen joined the new monastic orders and many people from England went to Ireland to participate in these exciting developments. Monasteries became the centres for art and teaching in the Irish community; the abbot was head of the house and so had the highest status, above bishops or priests. The abbot and monks were often lay people and married. Rivalries existed between monasteries, indeed they occasionally employed armies to fight against each other. By the seventh century, monasteries ranged in type from the most worldly, with a lay abbot running a prosperous business establishment, to the most devout and evangelical, such as those at Inishmurray in Sligo and at Iona near Mull.

Friction with the Roman church became more bitter when Celtic monasteries were set up on the continent by Columbanus and at Lindisfarne by Aidan. Several meetings were arranged to try to resolve the conflict of opinions; the best known, as it is reported by Bede, is the synod of Whitby which took place in 664. The major points of difference discussed were that the Celtic church, as opposed to Rome, had no diocesan organisation and no generally accepted monastic rule; and that it had different rituals and liturgy, a different tonsure and celebrated Easter at a different time. The difference over calculating

Easter was the most obvious to the general population, although perhaps not the most important. Opinion at Whitby was in favour of the Roman Easter and Roman practices. Thereafter the Celtic church gradually declined, although this took many years in the north and west of Britain.

On Lindisfarne, however, the effects were immediate. Bishop Colmán resigned in 664 rather than accept Roman practices. He returned to Ireland and established a monastery at Mayo. The next bishop, Tuda, also came from Ireland, but nevertheless followed the Roman Church. He, with many of his flock, died in a plague which swept over Northumberland the year after he took up office. Tuda was the last bishop from Ireland. The religious house on Lindisfarne was very much involved in the secular life of the Northumbrian kingdom. Bede has many stories of Aidan's influence over the kings and Colmán is also recorded as having resolved disputes for King Oswiu. As a mark of respect for Colmán on his resignation, the king appointed his nominee as abbot of Lindisfarne. This was how Eata came to the island from Melrose.

A vigorous ecclesiastical champion of the Roman Church in the north, at this time, was Wilfred. He took the opportunity given by the sudden death of Tuda to remove the bishopric from the island to York. Wilfred also engaged in an intensive building programme and erected famous churches at Hexham, York and Ripon. Eata was left in charge of the dismayed monastery of Lindisfarne as an abbot. The increase in religious activity in the north and the size of Northumberland led Archbishop Theodore of Canterbury to suggest that the area should be subdivided into three smaller bishoprics at Lindsey, York and either Hexham or Lindisfarne. New bishops were appointed at Lindsey, York and Hexham during the temporary absence of Wilfred, who had gone to Rome to complain to the pope about the division of his old see. He returned with the support of the pope, but the king of Northumbria, Ecgfrith, was determined to carry through the reforms of Theodore; he eventually banished Wilfred and created a fourth bishopric at Lindisfarne. Abbot Eata was made bishop in 678.

The bishop of Hexham was deposed in 684 and a synod convened to elect a new bishop. Theodore and Ecgfrith were responsible for the election of the Prior of Lindisfarne to the vacant position. This prior, Cuthbert, was a northern monk living the life of a hermit on the Farne Islands which he was reluctant to leave. So Bishop Eata offered to become the new bishop of Hexham whilst Cuthbert accepted the see of Lindisfarne.

CUTHBERT

Cuthbert was born in the region of the present-day Scottish border. Accounts of his life say that he had a foster mother, suggesting he was of noble parents. As a young man Cuthbert is recorded to have been on the northern banks of the Tyne, at Chester-le-Street and attending flocks of sheep near the river Leader. He grew up in the 640s, a period of considerable change and religious turmoil in Northumbria. He first decided to become a monk in 651 when about seventeen years old. Attracted by stories of the priest Boisil, Cuthbert entered the monastery of Old Melrose, where Eata was abbot; so started a friendship lasting many years. Melrose, although farther north than Lindisfarne, observed many of the Roman Benedictine rules. At once Cuthbert was noted as an enthusiastic follower of much stricter religious observances. He followed a mixture of Roman and ascetic Celtic rules throughout his life; during different stages of his career one aspect, Roman or Celtic, tended to be uppermost. The older he became the more he tended towards a withdrawn way of life.

Cuthbert went with Eata to Ripon for a time, but the Melrose monks returned home after the Synod of Whitby, and Cuthbert was made Prior of Melrose, achieving as much fame as his predecessor, Boisil, with his zeal in teaching and his missionary activities.

When Cuthbert was about thirty he was transferred by Eata to Lindisfarne as prior, and during this period, Eata was abbot of both Melrose and Lindisfarne. Once a Celtic house and now Roman in its practices, Lindisfarne appeared rather lax to Cuthbert. He introduced his mixture of Roman and Celtic rules, as used at Melrose, and once more outstripped all others with his religious zeal. He countered some initial local resistance by his understanding, example and repetition, and gradually won the respect and admiration of the monks. As at Melrose, he engaged in a great deal of pastoral work in the north.

Now the Celtic side of his nature asserted itself. He withdrew from participation in the affairs of the monastery to St Cuthbert's Island, just to the south-west of Lindisfarne. But the greater isolation of the island of Inner Farne, some seven miles away, was more attractive to him. Cuthbert needed to achieve a complete physical isolation and bodily subjugation to develop a deeper spiritual understanding. He started his hermit's life, which was to last over ten years on this occasion. The monks of Lindisfarne erected houses and an oratory for him and also sunk a well. He cultivated some barley and onions, but was generally looked after by the Holy Island monks whenever possible. Although he was geographically remote, the fame of this hermit spread throughout England and a constant stream of visitors came to see him. In time, he saw fewer and fewer people, and shut himself up in his small cell for longer and longer periods.

It was at this stage that Cuthbert became Bishop of Lindisfarne. He was then compelled to travel throughout his see and reports tell of him at Carlisle within twelve months of taking up office. He was bishop for two years and then resigned to return to his cell on Farne. Though only in his early fifties, his austere life had left its mark and he became ill after resuming his old isolated existence. He died within a year, on 20 March 687; despite his request to be buried on Farne, his body was removed to a stone coffin in the church at Lindisfarne and placed under the floor to the right of the altar.

Disinterments

The process of sanctification of Cuthbert began during the period 688–98, while his successor, Eadberht, was bishop. Miracles which had occurred near Cuthbert's person in life were recorded in relation to his remains, and the island church became a place of pilgrimage. The wealth they brought to Lindisfarne enabled Eadberht to give the wooden cathedral a new lead roof to replace the reed thatch.

The developing preoccupation with the sanctity of Cuthbert led to the first disinterment of his remains eleven years after his death, when they were found, miraculously, to be in a semi-mummified condition. This gave added impetus to the cult growing up around Cuthbert and prompted Eadberht to make a wooden coffin, with a carved exterior, to hold the remains.

These were again examined in 1104, 1537, 1827 and 1899. The last occasion was the only time a proper medical study was carried out; examination of the bones by Dr Selby Plummer revealed that Cuthbert was a muscular man, about 5ft 8in tall, who probably died of tuberculosis. Various personal objects belonging to the saint were removed during examinations of the coffin: some seventh-century cloth; jewellery, including his famous pectoral cross; and a bible, now known as the Stoney-hurst Bible.

A wooden inner coffin was also discovered; this was almost certainly the one made by Eadberht in 698. It was designed as a reliquary; the lid could be opened to reveal some of the saint's possessions, as well as the body itself. According to Bede, this was a 'light chest' made also to transport the remains of Cuth-bert. Reginald of Durham saw it in 1104 and commented that 'the whole of the exterior [was] engraved with the most wonderful carving ... minute and fine in its workmanship, [of] manifold forms of animals and flowers and the likeness of men'. By 1827 it had partly disintegrated, but it has been recon-structed and is on show in the library of Durham Cathedral.

55

The lid is inscribed with a full-length picture of Christ surrounded by the symbols of the four evangelists. The sides depict archangels, the Apostles and the Virgin. They are all labelled with runic versions of Latin words. The style is similar to the Lindisfarne Gospels, drawing together several distinct elements, but being basically Saxon in origin.

St Cuthbert's Isle

This small island, which is separated from Holy Island at high tide, was the site of Cuthbert's earliest retreats before he went to the Farnes and Eadberht, also, was in the habit of isolating himself there in Lent. There are the remains of some old buildings, mostly associated with a medieval chapel. The island was excavated by Sir William Crossman in 1888 and has

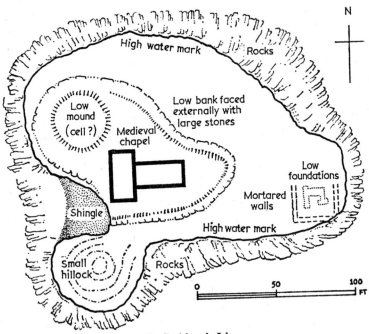

St Cuthbert's Isle

been surveyed later. The remains of a small and very old building to the south-east of the grassy part of the isle are visible, but have not been accurately examined. It is quite possible that this is the building used by Cuthbert and other bishops and monks as a place for solitary prayer and contemplation without being too far away from the cathedral. This would have made an acceptable compromise for Benedictines who would not like to follow strictly Celtic practices in such a matter.

NORTHUMBRIAN ART

The fame of Lindisfarne made the island and Northumbria one of the most important centres for art and learning in Britain. The early artistic expressions of the Saxons are demonstrated primarily in jewellery. The Sutton Hoo treasures and the Franks Casket display the basic elements of design: coils, serpents and trumpets. With the coming of Christianity, these same elements were carved in stone on cross shafts. Several fragments of stone cross shafts found on Holy Island date from the eighth and ninth centuries. Other discoveries include a stone grave cover, with an incised cross, and four small grave markers, three of which date from the earlier Saxon period and were excavated near the priory. The first was discovered in 1888 and, like the later finds, is made of local hard sandstone. It measures $8\frac{1}{4}$ × $6\frac{3}{4}$ × $1\frac{1}{2}$in and has a rounded top. On it is inscribed a cross with a male name *Aedberecht* in Hiberno-Saxon lettering. The second marker bears a cross and the female name *Osgyth* in both letters and runes; the third has a more elaborate cross, but is broken and the inscription is lost. These two were found in 1915 by the Office of Works; it is uncertain whether they even mark the site of a cemetery as no bones were found with any of these markers. The woman's name could mean that the earlier religious establishment had a nunnery attached, although there is no documentary evidence for this.

The fourth grave marker, which dates from the period after

the first Viking attack in 793, is unique in its representation of seven armed men on one side; six have their arms raised, brandishing swords or long handled axes. Carved in relief on the other side are a square-ended cross, two people in prayer, two hands, the sun and the moon. This might be a Saxon representation of attacking Vikings or defending Anglo-Saxons; the stylistic date is the ninth century.

THE LINDISFARNE GOSPELS

The Anglo-Saxon artists found the perfect medium for the full expression of their talents in the production of manuscripts and the copying and compilation of books. The finest book of the early Saxon period is the Lindisfarne Gospels—the earliest fully illuminated English book known, one of the most important art works of 'Dark Age' Britain and among the most splendid hand-written religious books in the world. There is no other English work comparable to its 22,800 lines of beautiful half uncial script, its magnificently coloured illustrations and specially illuminated 'carpet' pages. The 258 folio pages of vellum are in a remarkably good state of preservation.

The manuscript consists of the four gospels in a copy of a pure south Italian version of the vulgate, the Eusabian Canons and two epistles: one of Jerome and one of Eusabius. The books from which this copy was made may have been brought to Northumbria by Benedict Biscop after one of his five journeys to Rome. The story of the origin of the Lindisfarne Gospels is told by Aldred, later provost of Chester-le-Street, who in about 930 interlined an English translation or gloss into the manuscript. He also wrote a tailpiece or colophon as explanation. Part of the colophon states that:

> Eadfrith bishop of the Lindisfarne church he this book wrote, at first for God and St Cuthbert and all the saints in common who in the island are, and Ethilwold the Lindisfarne islanders bishop pressed it outside and bound it as well he could . . .

The words Aldred uses of Eadfrith are '*he this boc awrat*'; *awrat* is the past tense of the verb *awritan*, an Old English word which in pre-literate times meant 'to draw' and later 'to write'. Undoubtedly the illustrations, illuminations and calligraphy were all done by the same man, Eadfrith, probably before he became bishop in 698. The evidence of other sources suggests the book was produced in the years 696–8.

The gospels are important as well as beautiful, firstly because they demonstrate a major step in the evolution of the medieval manuscript form and, secondly, because they draw together widely divergent styles. The art is basically Saxon, although the influence of this art in later Celtic works led to the earlier mistaken assumption that this work was an Irish product. There are also significant Italian, Roman and Celtic influences.

The originals of the Lindisfarne Gospels are in the British Museum, but a facsimile copy was recently given to the parish church on Holy Island, where it can now be seen.

Many other manuscripts must have been produced by the monks of Lindisfarne, but only a few are known. However, the fame of Northumbrian scholarship at this time spread to the rest of Europe. A Saxon poem of the ninth century speaks of the calligrapher, 'Ultan: a blessed priest of the Scotic nation, who could adorn little books with elegant devices, in this art no modern scribe could rival him'. Ultan was probably a member of a religious house within the see of Lindisfarne.

THE VIKING ATTACKS

The greatest period of monastic life on Lindisfarne, which followed the death of Cuthbert, came to an end during the episcopate of Higbald, the eleventh bishop, when the Danes attacked the island in 793. This was the first recorded Danish attack on Britain and it may have been the fame of Lindisfarne that caused the Danes to direct their assault upon it. At this time Northumbria was the most powerful of the Saxon kingdoms, and the glory of the kings was matched by the holiness, learning and artistic achievements of the northern bishops.

In this raid, the monastery on the island was destroyed and those monks who did not escape perished. The Danes then moved south in search of other wealthy monasteries. The church was rebuilt, though no details of it are known. In the north of the island, under the sand dunes, two coins of this era were found; these were stycas: one of Ethelred of Northumbria's reign (840–5) and the other of Wigmund, Archbishop of York (851–4). They were discovered in 1845 close to some old buildings which had been unearthed by workmen making a wagonway near the Links, and were described by the lord of the manor, John Strangeways Donaldson Selby. There were two sets of stone foundations, one 312 by 341ft externally and with numerous cross walls; the stones were loose, inadequately shaped and without mortar. The coins were found near a second, smaller set of buildings, not fully described. These foundations could be Saxon, medieval or later in origin. Pits near the larger building could be associated with the production of kelp. Some of the stones were taken to make the wagonway, but most of the remains must still be under the sand awaiting rediscovery and further investigation.

The last Bishop of Lindisfarne was Eardulph who took office in 854. The Viking attacks were resumed along the north-east coast in 875, when Tynemouth Priory was razed to the ground and a party of Vikings headed north for Lindisfarne. The bishop decided to follow Cuthbert's dying instructions and remove his remains from the island. The monks took with them other valuable or venerable items, including the Lindisfarne Gospels, a Liber Vitae, the head of St Oswald and the bones of other bishops. The monastery was left to be destroyed.

The monks of Lindisfarne wandered over much of northern England and southern Scotland, carrying their priceless treasures with them. In 883 they settled at Chester-le-Street, where they remained for over a hundred years. Another Danish scare necessitated a series of moves, and the monks reached Ripon in 995. On their return north they found the defensive site at Durham and built the first cathedral there shortly afterwards.

During the period from 883 until the Norman Conquest, Lindisfarne remained in desolation; it is not mentioned in any documents nor have any archaeological remains been found dating from that time. The golden age of Holy Island was over.

4   RELIGIOUS LIFE ON
HOLY ISLAND

S T CUTHBERT'S remains were returned to Lindisfarne
for a brief period in the eleventh century, as William the
Conqueror prepared to take revenge on the Northumbrians
for the murder of a Norman noble, Robert Cumin. By March
1070, however, the monks had taken them back to Durham,
leaving the last Saxon Bishop of Durham to flee the country.
The first Norman bishop, Carileph, gave extensive properties to
the new Durham monastery, including Holy Island and much
of the nearby mainland. It was from this time that Lindisfarne
became known as 'The Holy Island', partly because of the
slaughter there by the Danes and partly because of the early
saints. For much of the medieval period the Benedictine house
of Durham had nine institutions linked to it; these included the
priories at Coldingham in Berwickshire and on the Farne
Islands, as well as Holy Island.

THE PRIORY

The earliest Norman influence on Holy Island was thought to
be the establishment of the priory, but Alan Piper of Durham
University has suggested that the island's church was built by
the Normans as a cult church to St Cuthbert and the other
saints, before a priory was contemplated. There are several
documentary and architectural reasons to support this theory.
One document records that no church existed on Holy Island

in 1093. Reginald, writing in 1165, states that Edward, another monk from Durham, erected the church on the island, new from its foundations with stone brought from the mainland.

The priory church

This was probably the priory church; the monk Edward is known as an active builder and architect working around 1122. Other evidence which suggests the church was not built as part of a priory is its grandiose style, which is not matched by the other priory buildings. The west door is unusually large; perhaps for ceremonial purposes. There was a door in the south aisle, giving access to what later became the cloisters; this was of no use in a priory and was later blocked up. The entrance to the church used as the 'night stair door' is also unusual in its siting. The lands given to the church were insufficient to maintain a normal priory, but would have been sufficient to support a popular site for pilgrimage. The church undoubtedly did become part of the priory, though perhaps not until fifty years after it was built.

The church was finished in the early twelfth century and, with the exception of late buttressing and a few windows, is entirely Norman in style. The building was originally planned with a short chancel and apse, but this was changed to a square-ended presbytery with three bays. There are two very short transepts, each with an apsidal chapel in the east wall. At the transept crossing, two piers, one of which remains, carried a tower. The nave consists of six bays with two aisles, north and south. It closely resembles the architectural work in Durham Cathedral, major cruciform piers alternating with circular ones —the latter of ornamented design, also found at Durham. The choir occupied the transept crossing, while the positions of the pulpit and rood screen are indicated respectively by marks in the stone in the north-west pier and the first circular pier to the north of the nave. The west front has an elaborate round-headed doorway. The lay public was, at one time, admitted through a small doorway in the north wall, which was blocked in the fifteenth century.

Monastic buildings

The surviving monastic buildings, all dating from some time after 1190, comprise those around the cloister and a more southerly outer court. The cloister was small and its surrounding buildings were designed to accommodate only a few monks. The original plan has been altered several times and by the fifteenth century there were no processional routes or covered walks. The refectory, to the south of the cloister, incorporated the south walk during fourteenth-century alterations. The buildings to the east and west of the cloister were fortified in the fourteenth century and these alterations obliterated other parts of the old cloister walks. Two-storeyed buildings to the east of the cloister included the dormitory and chapter house, while to the south others housed the refectory, which abutted the brewhouse and bakehouse to the west, and the prior's lodgings and other private rooms to the east. Most of this set of buildings date from the thirteenth century, while the remains of the brewhouse and bakehouse are fourteenth century, as are the buildings to the east of the prior's lodging which include an infirmary. The west side of the cloister is much earlier, being built between 1190 and 1210. The six small windows in the west wall of these buildings are still to be seen. The outer courtyard is mostly unaltered from when it was constructed in the early fourteenth century. It is surrounded by buildings, one of which encloses a well and others which may have been guest houses. There was also a burial ground for monks outside the precincts of the priory, probably due east of the priory church.

The monks of Lindisfarne

Holy Island Priory, after the Norman Conquest and before the Reformation, was by no means the independent and influential house of Anglo-Saxon times. There is no evidence, for

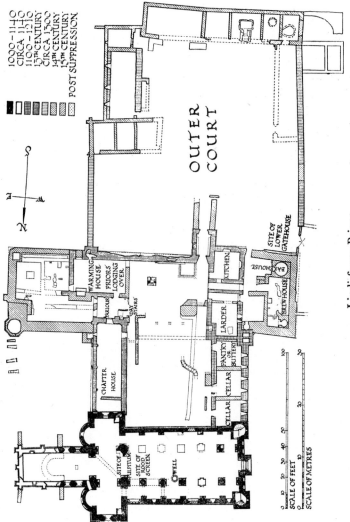

1000–1140
CIRCA 1140
1100–1210
13TH CENTURY
CIRCA 1300
14TH CENTURY
15TH CENTURY
POST SUPPRESSION

OUTER COURT

SITE OF LOWER GATEHOUSE

BACKHOUSE

BREWHOUSE

KITCHEN

LARDER

PANTRY OR BUTTERY

CELLAR

CELLAR

WARMING HOUSE

PRIORS LODGING OVER

PARLOUR

DAY STAIRS

CHAPTER HOUSE

SITE OF PULPITUM

SITE OF ROOD SCREEN

WELL

SCALE OF FEET

SCALE OF METRES

Lindisfarne Priory

example, that novices were ever trained there. Little or no parochial work was carried out by the prior and his monks either on the island or the mainland. Until the fourteenth century there were probably five monks on Lindisfarne at any one time. The Prior of Durham could, without episcopal consent, appoint priors and monks to the island and often dissident monks were sent there from the Durham fraternity for short periods of service. The long list of priors (see Appendix A) and the recurring names reflect the generally disagreeable isolation of Holy Island.

There are indications that by the early fourteenth century the monks traded in cloth, engaged in iron smelting, coal mining, quarrying, brewing, baking, fishing and lime burning. A small amount of farming was done on the island, including the growing of grass for hay; flax, hemp, beans, onions and leeks. Other income came from the wrecks of ships, although this source was often disputed with the bishopric.

The monks were ready to take up any speculative venture which might be profitable, even investing in foreign trade from time to time. On the island they let lodging rooms in property they owned; controlled property development, and collected rents and leases.

The annual accounts of the priory have survived in an almost unbroken sequence from 1326 until the dissolution of the monasteries in the sixteenth century. Before the wars with Scotland began during the thirteenth century, the annual income of the monks was around £200, but by 1328 it had fallen to £69. Their main source of income came from tithes and these were seriously curtailed by the destruction of many farms in Northumberland during the wars; subsequent fluctuations in the payment of tithes were brought about by the unstable prices of wheat and barley. By 1440 tithes brought in £34 and this dropped in the following year to £9 16s 8d.

In exchange for a fraction of the tithes, the priors placed the mainland area under the protection of a local landowner;

Page 67 Holy Island village: *(above)* aerial view from the west. In the right foreground is the churchyard and vicarage; in the centre the new council houses with St Coomb's farm to the top left. The sites of demolished cottages may be seen in the foreground; *(below)* the herring houses. One of the island's most recently modernised buildings showing the care taken when converting old properties

Page 68 (above) The lime kilns: this massive structure is to be renovated by the National Trust, which also owns the castle shown in the background; *(below)* stable sand dunes near the Snook tower and house. This was the site of a coal boring and later a military firing range

Walter of Goswick, for instance, acted as protector in 1314–15. During the wars with Scotland, the island itself was only attacked once—and that was before 1326, when William Prendergast removed baking and brewing equipment. Perhaps fear of St Cuthbert acted as a deterrent to border raiders; none the less the prior employed a watchman on the Snook.

Fortifications

During the fourteenth century considerable alterations were made to the priory to convert it into a fortified stronghold. The original gable, above the vault, on the west front of the priory church, was removed; the walls at each side were heightened and the roof raised. Two crossbow slits were made below the new gable. The south walk of the cloisters was obliterated by a mass of masonry. The prior's lodgings were also reconstructed as part of this general upheaval in 1341, which may have been when the rest of the rebuilding was undertaken.

Documents and excavation of the remains of the priory show that a new east wing was constructed and enclosed by a strongly built and fortified wall, with a half octagon tower at its north corner. A west wing, accommodating the brewhouse and bakehouse, was reconstructed, possibly after the destruction by William Prendergast and his followers. The walls here are very thick and at one time abutted a lower gatehouse which led into the outer courtyard. This newly constructed wing was mentioned in a list of articles owned by the priory in 1347. A fortified inner gatehouse between the cloisters and outer courtyard was also made—such a barbican being unique in English monastic buildings. The south and east walls of the outer courtyard were rebuilt or strengthened about this period.

The priory was thus changed from a regular Benedictine establishment into a fortified church. About 1416 the number of resident monks was reduced to two or three, while a greater part of the valuable items was taken to Durham, including the island's only bible and the Lindisfarne Gospels.

E

In 1437 there were five guns in the priory and by the end of the fifteenth century ten stockguns, five muskets and a crossbow.

The end of the monastic era

In the medieval period the island was the centre of local events for the north-east part of Northumberland. There was a market on the island, a safe harbour for ships and news must have come to the priory of events in the outside world. Royal ships and many merchant ships called regularly and whilst the Scottish border fighting continued life must have been eventful but largely undocumented. However, one event is recorded. In 1462, during the Wars of the Roses, Margaret, wife of Henry VI, was shipwrecked off the island and landed with 400 French troops. They took the small Yorkist garrison but were soon displaced by the troops of the Earl of Warwick.

The last century of the priory's existence is marked by many complaints to Durham from the prior about the laxity among the monks. In 1465 two of them, Robert Knowle and Robert Billington, were accused of wearing linen shirts, frequenting taverns, playing dice, swearing, and uttering prohibited jests, contrary to the Benedictine rule.

The last prior, Thomas Sparke, was made a suffragan bishop and given the cell of Holy Island, or what remained of it, for the rest of his life. This gift, made by the new dean and chapter of Durham, consisted of far fewer acres than were initially assigned to the Lindisfarne cell. In 1537 Sparke held the priory itself, two orchards known as Baggot and Coldingham Walls, thirteen small gardens and fifteen cottages. With this list of property ended nearly 500 years of Benedictine monastic life.

MEDIEVAL CHAPELS

There may have been three small chapels on Holy Island. One, recorded today in the name of St Coomb's Farm, appears in historical documents as an old field name near the modern water tower, but not in any early church records. A second may have existed on the Heugh, but this has yet to be substantiated as the site is awaiting excavation. The third, on Hob Thrush, was known as the Chapel of St Cuthbert in the Sea; for this small building, near the site of the cell used by Cuthbert, there is both documentary and archaeological evidence.

This site, excavated by Sir William Crossman in 1888 and resurveyed more recently, consists of the foundations of a cell or ante-chapel some 28ft long by 15ft wide, the chapel itself, adjoining it and aligned to the east, being 24ft long by 12ft wide. The walls were 2–3ft thick and made of local dolerite rock.

There is also a rough breakwater to the east of the chapel. At the south-west corner of the island is a fragmentary building which may have been another cell; part of this appeared to be pre-medieval in construction and could be the cell of Cuthbert. A list of the contents of the priory in 1533 notes the contents of this chapel: a few church ornaments and vestments with images of St Cuthbert and St Thomas, a crucifix and nine linen altar cloths.

THE PARISH CHURCH

The parish church, 52ft due west of the old priory church, is dedicated to St Mary the Virgin. It originally consisted of an aisleless chancel and nave. The earliest parts of the fabric are the three late twelfth-century arches on the north side of the nave. The columns are of red stone and the connecting ribs of each arch are of alternate courses of red and white stone—a unique feature of the church.

The church was considerably enlarged in the thirteenth century, when an additional arch was constructed, connecting the old north arcade to a new west front; the south arcade and chancel arch also belong to this period. The columns of the south aisle, 10ft 4in in height, are not symmetrically placed in relation to those of the north aisle, being 1ft 2in shorter. The two aisles produced by these arcades were probably chapels in medieval times. The chancel arch is 11ft 6in wide but has been altered at a later date. It leads into a beautiful long chancel some 49ft long and 17ft 3in wide. The chancel has several early English windows; three stepped lancets at the east end, and other lancets and smaller lights in the north and south walls. The other windows in the church are largely later medieval modifications of early types. Recent renovations in the church have shown that many of the windows have relieving arches. The church now consists of a nave 56ft by 19ft 6in with two aisles and two westerly porches, the older one of the two, in the north once acted as a mortuary, but since 1886 has served as a vestry.

There is a piscina at the south-east angle of the south aisle, and three ancient aumbries—one on the north side of the chancel near the most easterly light. Other church furniture is much later in date; the font, said to come from Durham, dates from the seventeenth or eighteenth century, and the altar slab too is relatively modern. By the middle of the seventeenth century some efforts were made to repair the church. Thomas Shaftoe, the parliamentary governor of the island, refurnished the interior—by then nearly devoid of furniture—donating a carved oak pulpit inscribed 'TS May 3rd 1646' and box pews, which were there two centuries later. Dr George Johnston, visiting the island in 1854, noted that 'The church is cold, damp and musty within; the walls are covered with green mould'. The bell-cote is supported by two massive buttresses connected high up by an arch, built in 1723. At the same time the 'battlements' were repaired, the south porch constructed and a seat made for the clerk. The work cost £24 and the stone required was taken from the old priory.

Plans made in 1836 for extensive modifications to the interior did not get under way until 1860 when funds became available. All the Commonwealth woodwork was then removed, the floor between the nave and chancel was levelled, and the walls were plastered. The pitch of the roof of the nave may have been altered at this time; it was originally flat. New pews to seat about 300 people were added, as well as a new pulpit. All that remains of the oak of Thomas Shaftoe is the lectern made from the old pulpit. During the repair work a carved stone coffin lid was found and fixed in the wall of the chancel. On it is a cross, a mitre-shaped shield and a sword; it has no date or inscription.

All the glass in the church is modern. Some is in the form of memorial windows; two were given by Alexander Wilson dated 1905, in memory of his wife Eliza. There are three memorial tablets on the walls in the south aisle, commemorating John Hemsworth, Jane Moffett and John Askew, and one on the north wall of the chancel to Ann Jones, wife of the castle governor.

In the chancel are four large hatchments—coats of arms of individuals painted and framed at the time of their death—commemorating John Askew, who died in 1794; Sir Carnaby Haggerston, who died in 1831; his wife, who died eight years later, and Henry Collingwood Selby, who died in 1839 at the age of ninety-one. The north aisle, adjacent to the Haggerston hatchments and known as the Haggerston aisle, contains several other memorials to that family.

This aisle was made into a chapel once more in 1939, when it was dedicated to St Peter. A slab near the reading desk is dedicated to Sir William Reed of Fenham, who died in 1604; he was the lease holder of the dean and chapter. His grave is inscribed '*Contra vim mortis non est medicamen in hortis*' (against the power of death there is no cure in the garden).

A small organ, originally from a church in County Durham, stands at the eastern end of the south aisle. The church plate consists of two old silver pieces. One is a cup 9in high and 4in in diameter at the mouth. It is inscribed '*Anno 1579 Holy Island*', but the hall marks indicate that it was remade by Eli Bilton of Newcastle in 1712 from an Elizabethan original. The other piece is a plate or paten 7½in in diameter; it has a moulded edge 2¾in high and is on a short stem with an open base. Inscribed '*Anno 1789 Holy Island*', it was made by Langland and Robertson of Newcastle in 1788 and presented to the church on 7 October 1789 by the Rev Dr Pointz, a prebendary of Durham.

Since the 1950s, when the vicarage was rebuilt, the church has been gradually restored and repaired. Much of the plaster put on in 1860 has been removed and the old stone work pointed. The removal of some of the pews which crowd the church will make the interior much more attractive. A new and notable feature of the chancel, and now in front of the altar, is a carpet designed and made by eighteen island ladies. The design was taken, appropriately, from one of the 'carpet' pages in the Lindisfarne Gospels.

THE ANGLICAN MINISTRY

The original parish of Holy Island, founded in medieval times, once included these townships and chapelries in North Northumberland: Fenham, Goswick, Kyloe, Fenwick, Buckton, Beal, Berrington, Lowlin, Lowick and Samshouse, Baremoor, Gatherick, Howburn, Bowsden, Ancroft, Cheswick, Scremerston, Haggerston, Tweedmouth, Ord and Murton. As the years went by, the chapelries became parishes in their own right or effectively exercised parochial rights, so that Holy Island parish became smaller and smaller. In 1862 the diocese of Newcastle was founded and the care of the parish passed to a new bishop. By the end of the nineteenth century all the mainland parts of the parish had been lost; the last to be detached were Fenham, Fenwick, Broomhouse and Goswick. For over seventy years, therefore, the vicars of Holy Island have been responsible for the welfare of the island only; during that time the nature of the ministry has changed from one purely concerned with the inhabitants to one embracing tourists, pilgrimages and many aspects of church unity.

A recent church venture has been the establishment of a Christian Centre on the island. This long-cherished concept of the vicar, the Rev Denis Bill, was realised when Marygate House was purchased in 1969. A warden is now in residence and the house is open for use by groups of all denominations as a retreat, a study centre and a place for conferences.

All the churches on the island have developed a close association over the last few years, thanks to the ministers and lay workers. Marygate House is one way in which this is expressed. Another ecumenical aspect is evident in the many pilgrimages to the island—either individual ones or well-organised affairs involving thousands of people walking across the sands and attending a service in the priory ruins. The frequency and popularity of these pilgrimages are measures of the Christian fellowship which exists on the island today.

THE PRESBYTERIAN CHURCH

Some of the early Anglican curates—for example, William Mitton—were Scotsmen, whilst others must have had Scottish sympathies, such as John Ainslye, who allowed John Knox to preach on the island in 1550, when it is recorded that a quarter of the island's fifty inhabitants were 'Scotchmen'. A letter from the vicar James Robertson to the Bishop of Durham, written in 1778, highlighted a rift between the Anglican and Scottish churches:

> James Huet being a dissenter from the Church of England and teaching school there without licence . . . was charged for—his wilful and obstinate neglect in not bringing the children to church—and neglecting to teach them the church catchecisms. He seems determined to continue in the office of schoolmaster at all hazard—being thereto encouraged by a few unprincipled and ill disposed persons.

In 1736 there were forty-three Presbyterian families on the island out of nearly 200; by 1793 there were only eleven families out of eighty; in that year, Lancelot Wilson, the vicar, recorded that most of the Presbyterians attended the Anglican services.

Many known Presbyterians are recorded in the parish registers. However, occasional illegal 'Scottish' marriages were performed throughout the eighteenth century and those known to the vicar—taking place between 1799 and 1822—are recorded in a separate part of the Anglican registers. One such marriage on 9 March 1822, between Robert Young and Elizabeth Newton, was solemnised 'on the centre of the Union Bridge fronting the borders of Scotland by Tweed Hill' and one John Forster officiated. Others took place at Coldstream and at the Lamberton Old Toll.

The first Presbyterian minister to work on the island was Alexander Moody, who came as a probationer in December 1832 at the invitation of Mr Buchan of Kelloe. He was in his early twenties and a popular preacher—all the more so after his help with a cholera epidemic in November 1834; the disease spread from a foreign ship in the harbour and lasted six weeks. When he left the island in the spring of 1835 to work in Edinburgh, he was not replaced, but after his departure there was some non-conformist preaching by Primitive Methodists.

The Presbyterians formally included Lindisfarne in the United Presbyterian Church of Scotland mission in 1860, when two local ministers shared services on the island. A building was rented and by 1872 there were twenty-nine church members; two years later a cottage opposite the Lindisfarne Hotel was converted into a mission hall. In 1876 the church passed to the care of the newly formed Presbyterian Church of England. The hall proved too small for the growing congregation and a church eventually came into being through the efforts of the resident missionary, Mr Farquarson. Sir William Crossman donated the site and stone from the island quarry, while £800 was raised from other sources. Built in a simple 'early English' style, it measures 36ft by 23ft; there is a vestry at the eastern end and a small porch at the main entrance in the west front. The bell, the font, an American organ and the communion set were all gifts. The church was opened on 19 May 1892 and dedicated to St Cuthbert. The first elders of this new permanent church were a Mr Morton, George Markwell, George Simpson, John Smith and Alfred Welsh. The Misses Morton of Rose Cottage housed successive ministers to the island. Up to 1970 there had been only two organists: Thomas Markwell for thirty years and Mrs Tough for forty-eight years.

Most of the early ministers were probationers and so only stayed a short while. No regular minister has ever been appointed to the church due to lack of funds and accommodation. Services since the last war have been on a fortnightly basis and a friendly relationship has developed with the Anglican church. Church membership has fallen over the last century from sixty or so to about twenty; largely as the result of the general decline in population. The church is now part of the United Reformed Church.

The Presbyterian church is a small but important aspect of life on Holy Island, perpetuating an association between the inhabitants and Scotland that has existed for many centuries.

THE ROMAN CATHOLIC CHURCH

The Durham diocesan record books and visitation returns for the eighteenth and early nineteenth centuries record that only one or two Roman Catholic families lived on the island. Since the destruction of the priory, there has been no systematic mention of any connection between the Roman Church and the island. Some priests and many other Roman Catholics were buried on the island and appear in the parish registers; for example, an entry under the date 30 May 1781: 'Francis Diggs a Roman Catholic Priest of Barrington was buried'.

During the late nineteenth century there were many Roman

Catholic pilgrimages to the island; on 11 August 1887, for instance, 7,000 pilgrims walked over the sands to commemorate the twelfth centenary of St Cuthbert.

Lindisfarne House and its large garden was given to the Roman Catholic church by the Salvins of Croxdale during the latter part of the nineteenth century. At first the house was let to a series of tenants, while a small chapel holding about fifteen people was built adjacent to the house. This chapel was dedicated to Our Lady and St Aidan in 1890. By the early 1950s, it was in need of repair and, under the direction of Thomas Cahill of Alnwick, it was enlarged into an adjacent coach house and given a pebble-dashed and dressed stone exterior. The chapel is served by the priest from St Edward's church at Lowick and is open for mass on most Sundays from June to September.

Lindisfarne House is owned by the Trustees of the Hexham and Newcastle Diocese. Formerly run by the Hexham and Newcastle Northern Bretherens Fund as a rest and holiday home for the diocesan clergy, it is now used by the Hexham and Newcastle Diocesan Rescue Society as a family group home for deprived or homeless children; the groups use the house in turn at weekends and during school holidays. The garden at the rear of the house was grassed over after the last war and from 1954 acted as a camp site for boys, administered by the St Vincent de Paul Society. The camp's marquees and tents were replaced in the early 1970s by a permanent hall, which is used for eight weeks each year and can accommodate up to a hundred children.

Today there are only one or two Roman Catholic families on the island, but it seems fitting that the Roman church should retain a link with the place described in a Roman Catholic booklet in 1954 as 'the Holiest place in Britain'.

5   THE ISLAND AND ITS PEOPLE

LINDISFARNE was originally completely owned by the Norman bishops of Durham as the oldest patrimony of St Cuthbert. A small part of the island was given to the Priory of Durham and eventually became their cell on Holy Island. Other freeholds were given from time to time; for example, Bishop Robert de Insula gave an area of land in 'Lamesete' to the Priory of Coldingham on which to build a rest house. This may have been a part of an early medieval attempt to form a town on Holy Island. The naming of the village as a 'town' and the fact that such a small place was made into a medieval borough tend to confirm this. The plan failed, possibly because the Scottish wars made the island less attractive. Only the area around the village was enclosed and farmed; the rest of the island appears to have been a featureless waste of rough grass and sand. One part of this—the rabbit warren on the Snook—was most valuable, however; although the priors of Holy Island were allowed to take rabbits, the rest were strictly controlled for the benefit of the bishops in Durham. The bishop's bailiff was based at Norham and made counts of the rabbits three times a year.

At the dissolution, the priory owned fifteen cottages, thirteen gardens and two orchards, together with some pasture land. Many of these pieces of land gradually became freehold properties, as did some of the small parcels of land belonging to the crown. These added to the freehold properties in existence in medieval times.

79

James Raine, in his *History of North Durham*, says that an examination of the medieval Holy Island records shows all the leading families in Northumberland—Ord, Grey, Strangwis, Reaveley and many others—as being property owners on the island. The freeholds gradually came into the hands of owner occupiers: freeholders or stallengers with rights to fish, cut thatch and graze cattle. It was from these stable island people that the ancestors of the modern population emerged. The medieval burgesses performed official functions in relation to the Saturday market; they were committed to the island for their livelihood and tended to form its core community, unique in their island town and a law unto themselves.

Sir William Reed of Fenham recorded, on 1 May 1592, a detailed examination of the evidence of the freehold ownership on the island. In all, eighteen freehold properties were listed; each freeholder produced evidence to his rights, and in many cases this was traced back many generations: Jeremy Gardner held a property east of Piet Hill from a direct ancestor, Thomas Gardner, the original deed being dated 1356; Thomas Patterson owned a house in Marygate purchased from Thomas Haggerston in 1568, and James Lilburn gave a house and garden on Piet Hill to his son William in 1518.

The last prior, Bishop Sparke, sub-let the lease he had been given by the dean and chapter of Durham to the king's surveyor of victuals at Berwick. By 1550, the priory church and other buildings were converted for use as store houses for a naval victualling station. The bakehouse and brewhouse were both functioning to provide food for the navy. The entire structure, however, had not been repaired and the south-east corner of the brewhouse was in a dangerous condition. Several of the rooms had been split up into smaller compartments by the insertion of wooden partitions. The priory church was still in use as a store house in 1560, according to one of Queen Elizabeth I's survey books of Norham and Islandshire.

Sir William Reed was granted the lease of the priory, its land

and houses in 1564, to be taken up on the death of Bishop Sparke. This occurred in 1571 and William Reed's son, also William, held the lease until 1613. When James I of England came to the throne, he forced the Bishop of Durham to grant the royalties of Norham and Islandshire to George Hume, despite the existence of a bishop's leasee. In this way the crown lease was founded and the bishops of Durham lost control of the island.

By 1613 the crown lease was held by Lord Walden; in that year he asserted his rights of ownership over the entire island, including the old priory lands. He did this by removing the lead from the roof of the priory, its bells and whatever else he could find. He transported his spoils by ship, which was ironically lost in a storm with all its cargo. Ownership of the priory and much land and property on the island then fell to the Earls of Suffolk and a series of later crown leasees.

Priory ruins

Nothing was done with the ruinous and despoiled priory from the middle of the sixteenth century. Stones from the ruins were incorporated into all manner of buildings on the island. The old brewhouse-bakehouse complex was repaired for a time to be used as a residence and office for the crown leaseholder. The decline of the priory ruins continued until the early nineteenth century, when the crown leasee of the time ordered that the ruins should be made safe and tidied up. The first serious excavation of the remains was carried out by Sir William Crossman in 1888, who also made the first plan of the ruins. The ruins were eventually handed over to the forerunner of the Office of Works, who carried out further excavations in the twentieth century; they have now been considerably restored and are administered by the Department of the Environment, being supervised by a full time guide. An architectural and historical description of the ruins by the late A. Hamilton Thompson was published as a booklet by Her Majesty's Stationery Office.

The significance of the defence of Holy Island may have been to provide a safe harbour rather than primarily as a strong point against border raids. The harbour was used as a staging post for royal ships and fleets, and Edward Balliol is recorded as having spent the winter of 1335–6 on Holy Island after the battle of Culbhean. After the dissolution, the authorities had to find an alternative site to defend the harbour and hold the east flank of the border. In 1542 two temporary bulwarks were built to fulfil the old task of the decaying priory. They were constructed by Robert Rooke of Berwick and repaired in 1544.

The castle

In 1548–9 Thomas Holcrofte and an engineer were directed to find a site for further fortifications and the construction of the castle began. It was finished by 1550, when a survey records 'the fort of Beblowe, within the Holy Island, lyeth very well for the defence of the haven theire'. The fort was equipped with such old weapons as sakirs, falcons, culverins and demi-culverins. With its storehouses and naval victualling depot at the priory nearby, it remained an important garrison and haven for the support of Berwick.

In 1559 the permanent force consisted of a captain, two master gunners, a master's mate and twenty soldiers. Thereafter the castle was one of the few permanent garrisons in England, having regular soldiers stationed there until 1819. Although the site became far less important after the accession of James I of England, the continual replacement and activity of the soldiers formed an appreciable link between the island and the outside world, carrying on another function of the old priory. Less welcome were the diseases they brought to the island. Between 1 May and 23 June 1639, thirty-three soldiers were buried; an entry in the parish registers states that 'about

82

this tyme were sundrie sogers buried', so the total was probably much higher. Soldiers were also drowned in the Low as a result of their inability to judge the tide:

> September 2 1724 Richard Flatcher serjeant in Captain Charles Weddell company being lost in the Tyde was buried.

Although many of the captains of the castle did not live on the island, one of them, Henry Jones, had close associations with it. The memorial stone to his wife, Ann, is in the chancel of St Mary's church. He was succeeded in 1629 by his son-in-law, Robert Rugg, a character well known for his generous hospitality, his extraordinary stories and his enormous 'bottle' nose. Sir William Brereton noted the nose when he visited Holy Island in 1635. He also noted that there was a 'dainty little fort' which had 'neat, warm and convenient rooms'.

On 5 April 1643, a Roman Catholic missionary to Scotland, Father Gilbert Blackhal was storm bound on the island. He recounts how another ship was wrecked close by and how the minister of the parish—William Mitton—and a gentleman dwelling near the island, fought for a casset (cask) full of castor (beaver) hats with gold hat bands and 'the minister did sore wound the gentleman'. Rugg lost no opportunity to elaborate this tale and went into details of how the inhabitants of the island prayed for and obtained wrecks.

Rugg and his garrison were not paid for long periods during the troubled times before the Civil War broke out. At one stage he wrote a 'rhyming' letter to King Charles:

> Where Lindisfarne and Holy Island stand,
> These worthless lines sends to your worthie hands,

He then asked for his pay due to him over the previous sixteen months and ended:

> The great commander of the Gormorants,
> The geese and ganders of these hallowed lands.

83

Rugg received no pay and eventually surrendered the island to parliamentary forces.

Colonel Shaftoe, who was made the governor of the castle in 1645, had similar difficulty in obtaining his pay and had received none for his post when he died in 1646. Because of increasing Royalist activity in the area, Parliament reinforced the garrison shortly after the new military commander, Captain Batton, arrived. The Royalists asked Batton to change sides under promise that he and his troopers would receive pay. Batton refused and the island was besieged for some time; relief forces were sent from Newcastle and the island held out.

Steel End fort

In 1675 a 'platform and redoutte' was built at Steel End to secure the defence of the harbour. This may have been the result of Dutch privateering attacks on the east coast. The small fort was designed by Daniel Collingwood and Robert Trollopp. It comprised an outer crenellated platform looking south and east above which was a strongly walled diamond shaped enclosure with three small turrets in the wall. In the centre was a strong point of several storeys, having a steeply sloping roof. All that now remains of this structure is the lower storey of the strong point.

Decline of the castle

In 1715, two men, Lawrence Errington and his nephew, captured the castle for the Old Pretender. The total castle garrison then consisted of seven men; only two of them were on duty at the time, and were easily ejected. The intruders raised the Jacobite flag and awaited reinforcements from the mainland. Unfortunately a force of troops loyal to the English crown arrived first and took them prisoner, although they managed to escape some days later.

The garrison dwindled in size and was withdrawn in 1819,

Page 85 (above) The two fishwives – Sarah Cromarty and Bessie Morris – and their donkeys, mentioned in the poem on page 95; *(below)* an advertisement by the postmaster around the turn of the century showing the typical mode of transport to the island and one of the refuge boxes along the Pilgrims' Way

Conveyances between Holy Island and Beal.

APPLY TO

obert Bell, Grocer, Coal Merchant, &c.,

POST OFFICE, HOLY ISLAND, BEAL.

rams: "BELL, HOLY ISLAND."

Page 86 (above left) The Lough drain replaced a much larger stream that entered the Ouse further to the west than the modern drain and sluice system into which the field drains now pass. The picture shows the typical featureless appearance of the centre of the island; (above right) Popple Well, near the Iron Rails, was the most popular of the island wells until the 1950s when piped water was provided; (below) the dune slacks have a unique flora of their own. This photograph shows clusters of marsh helleborine, an orchid

being replaced by naval men acting as coastguards, who were
there in 1841. By 1851 the castle had been made into a civilian
coastguard station; the three coastguards who were billeted
there later went to live in the village. By 1861 the castle had
become the headquarters of the Northumberland Volunteers
and was occupied by a small regular staff of soldiers until the
1880s. In 1882 the old guns in the castle were replaced by three
rifled pieces, and some time after this the building was abandoned and fell into a ruinous condition.

Restoration

When Edward Hudson and Peter Anderson Graham, the
founder and editor of *Country Life*, visited the castle towards the
end of the last century, they saw its possibilities. Hudson purchased the castle from the Crown in 1902 and persuaded the
architect Edward Lutyens to restore it. He designed the castle
as it is today and made it far more impressive and romantic
than the original building.

From a ruin which at one time had three levels or batteries,
and two separate buildings, the east and west guardhouses, he
created a comfortable country house with nine bedrooms and
several other rooms, while at the same time retaining or improving the external appearance of the castle. The lower
battery is entered by a ramp on the south side and a portcullis
door which leads on to the lower, eastern battery. The building
itself is entered by a door leading into a large hall with the two
principal living rooms beyond, the dining-room and the ship
room. The upper battery was made into two more bedrooms.
Lutyens designed the windows, fireplaces, some furniture,
doors, locks, latches, the panelling and the beams. The rest of
the furniture was chosen at the time and is mainly seventeenth
century English and Flemish oak.

The castle was sold in the early 1920s to a banker, O. T. Falk,
who resold it after a few years to Sir Edward Stein, a merchant
banker. He and his sister, Gladys, used the castle as a family

holiday home until he gave it to the National Trust in 1944. Sir Edward remained as tenant until his death and his sister occupied it until she died in 1968. The castle remains occupied and in summer visitors are conducted round the main rooms.

THE CASTLE GARDEN

One of Lutyens' early patrons was Miss Gertrude Jekyll, the leading garden designer of her day, who co-operated with the architect on many projects, including the construction of a garden for Holy Island castle. For this purpose, she and Lutyens adapted an old walled enclosure, which may have been a sheep pen and was first noted on the Ordnance Survey maps in the mid-nineteenth century. Two of the old field walls were re-positioned to form an oddly shaped rectangle, leaving a set of walls 83ft × 88ft along the south and east aspects, but only 72ft × 67ft along the west and north sides, with perspective lines leading to featureless fields to the north.

Gertrude Jekyll had the supremely difficult task of planting this quadrilateral area so that it appeared a different shape when viewed obliquely from the castle. Her original plans have been copied and many of her plants identified by Michael Tooley of Durham University. The garden was probably constructed some time after 1912. The east side was to be used to grow vegetables for the castle, whilst the rest of the area was to comprise a wide variety of shrubs, herbs and flowering plants. The central bed was of scarlet and red gladioli, lobelia and geranium contrasted with a background of *Sedum telephium*.

The National Trust had hoped to replant the garden with the flowers and shrubs originally used by Miss Jekyll, but many of the hybrids are no longer in existence and it is financially impossible to plant many annuals. Many perennials and shrubs have been retained in their original position, however, and the general intention of Miss Jekyll of startling contrast has been retained throughout. The plants retained include delphinium, belladonna, *Helianthus tomentosus, Althea rosea, Fuschia magellanica, Jasminium nudiflorum* and *Stachys lanata.* The new garden, when finished, will enhance the National Trust properties on the island as well as providing a significant addition to the history of English gardening.

THE POPULATION

The number of people living on Holy Island has fluctuated over the years and must have been low after the dissolution. The border surveys of the last half of the sixteenth century all note the poverty of the village inhabitants and the disrepair of the property. The 1560 report, for example, records that the village is 'all sett with fishers, very poore, and is a markett town on ye Saturday, how beit it is little used'. At that time there were thirty-three householders on the island.

By 1601 a church tax on householders revealed forty taxable persons on the island and much the same in 1631. The number of inhabitants appears to have increased considerably by 1666 when the hearth tax returns record eighty-eight individual householders. This increase in population was due partly to the good fishing in the area and partly to the success of the kelp industry. Kelp results from seaweed burnt in pits and was once used as an agricultural fertiliser. It is mentioned specifically in many of the island leases, but was never noted in medieval accounts. It ceased to be profitable towards the end of the eighteenth century.

With the waning of the kelp trade and fishing, the population started to decline. In 1728 there were only twenty-four free-holders and a few stallengers. In 1736, when Bishop Chandler's visitation returns note just over 200 families living in Holy Island parish—this included the mainland areas—the island population was probably just over 100 families. By the 1760s many young people had moved away and, on 1 November 1765, several islanders were drowned, including two members of the Cromarty family, when four fishing boats were lost at sea in a freak storm. The impoverishment of the island meant that, contrary to the usual custom of maintaining their independence, some freeholders gave up their rights to people from the mainland.

The eighteenth century was also marked by an increase in lawlessness, no doubt partly due to the prevailing poverty. Fights between customs officials and 'pirates' are recorded and in 1760 the lord of the manor requested an Admiralty cutter to be stationed at the island. This request was not granted, although Lindisfarne acted as a shore station for customs officials and coast guards for many years.

By the 1790s the number of inhabitants had started to increase once more. The enclosure of the main part of the island met with strong resistance, partly because the first division of the common was a bad attempt and the whole process had to be repeated. By 1794 the island was gradually emerging from its pitiful state; Hutchinson records that the village consisted of 'a few irregular houses, two or more of which are inns and the rest inhabited by fishermen', and that it had been improved of late by the construction of new houses.

There had been a schoolmaster on the island for most of the eighteenth century; and a school and schoolmaster's house were built in 1796 with funds raised by public subscription. School facilities were improved over the next twenty years and some endowments given towards their upkeep.

The parish registers show an enormous increase in births starting in the early nineteenth century and reaching a peak about the middle of the century. The exact number of parish inhabitants now became known, thanks to the official census, which started in 1801, and to an enthusiastic vicar who counted the island population on several occasions. In 1797 the population was 364, and Hodgson noted that it was 379 in 1798 and 'it had formerly been much larger'. Another local count took

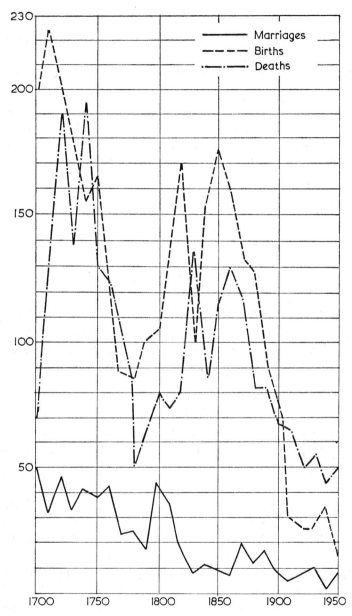

The number of births, marriages and deaths recorded in the parish registers for ten-year periods from 1700 to 1950

place in 1810 when there were 374 islanders, plus thirty soldiers at the castle.

The population increased rapidly in the first half of the nineteenth century, with a considerable inflow of people resulting from a new-found prosperity brought about by the industrial revolution. In 1841, there were 497 people on the island; in 1851, 553, and in 1861 a peak of 614 was reached. Over the next hundred years the number fell to 190:

1871	573
1901	405
1911	359
1931	287
1951	238
1961	190

Seven islanders died in World War I, a fine memorial by Lutyens being erected on the Heugh. Sixty Lindisfarne inhabitants served in the armed forces in World War II, and three more names were added to the war memorial.

INDUSTRY

A period of industrial enterprise in the early nineteenth century resulted in a new commercial prosperity. Coal, freestone and limestone, which had been taken from Lindisfarne since the Middle Ages, were in greater demand than ever before. At the same time herring in ever-increasing numbers appeared in the north-eastern coastal waters, which the islanders sold to Britain's expanding industrial population, and there was a growing market too for the inshore shellfish trade.

The island's prosperity was marked in several ways: a new market cross was given by Mr Selby in 1828; the main drain from the Lough was redug in 1820, and several hundred pounds were spent on the National School in 1870. A library with a

reading room was built and endowed by Sir William Crossman's family in the 1870s and by 1884 it held over 2,000
volumes; the daily papers were provided, as well as shipping
journals. The William Markwell charity was set up by a wealthy
expatriate, partly for educational service and partly to give two
guineas to the vicar each year to preach a sermon known as the
Markwell sermon. A second island charity comes from the will
of Mr Robert Crossman who died in 1883; he left a sum of
money to be distributed to the library, needy fisher families or
to help with church repairs.

The economic successes attracted further schemes to the
island. In the 1860s a proposal to connect it permanently with
the mainland was strongly resisted by the inhabitants and
finally quashed. A proposed railway branch line to the island,
ending in a jetty and pier with promenades, likewise came to
nothing.

Quarrying

In the 1780s there was a scheme to ship coal to Holy Island
and export burnt lime on the return journey; various projects
along these lines continued for nearly a century. In 1846, permission was granted to erect larger limeworks and extend the
enterprise to brick and tile making; although the latter notions
came to nothing, the result was an extension of the pier and
wagonway near Chare Ends, built about 1840, connecting a
quarry near the north shore to the lime works west of the Links.
A later scheme involved the erection of the large lime kilns near
the castle in the 1860s by a Dundee firm. The project was to
remove a greater part of the limestone coves on the north shore
and transport it by a wagonway along the east coast to the
limekilns and thence to a wooden jetty south-west of the castle
and to the ships. A few of the old wooden piers of this jetty can
still be seen.

In 1861 thirty-nine men were employed in limeworking and
carting—20 per cent of the adult male population—but this had

fallen to 14 per cent by 1871. Five vessels carried the coal and lime between the island and Dundee. By the early twentieth century, all the quarrying had ceased; the kilns and workmen's huts were falling into disrepair and being covered with sand.

The Carron Iron Company from Scotland removed nodular ironstone from the coastline during the early part of the nineteenth century. A coal mine was in existence on the Snook by 1791, but a more serious attempt to extract coal was made by Mr Selby in 1840 when the tower at the Snook was built. The project was not very successful and had been abandoned by 1875.

Fishing

In the first half of the nineteenth century, fishing was the dominant feature of island life. In 1794 ten or twelve small boats were in use in the summer, and by 1826 there were thirteen herring boats in operation, involving fifty-two men. By the 1850s and 1860s half the adult population was occupied in fishing and allied trades. George Johnston noted that the village streets were piled with shells, fishing lines and household ashes, producing a most disagreeable smell. The landing place was filthy and it was difficult to approach the boats without treading on garbage. Seventeen to twenty boats were engaged in the white-fish trade, also taking crab and lobster; and three other boats collected shellfish exclusively. Salmon nets were placed to the north of the Snook, and mussels and limpets picked regularly as bait. Periwinkles were sent to the south for human consumption; in 1854 over a hundred sacks were gathered in the first five months.

In 1859 Walter White records a similar combination of industry and dirt because of the herring fisheries. The herrings were cured in a large converted storehouse and many were then exported to the Baltic ports. At the peak of the herring boom, over thirty boats fished out of the island, but by 1875 the number had fallen to sixteen. That year, two decked boats were in use for the first time. The advent of the steam drifter and the decline in the numbers of herring finally killed the trade.

Two local characters of the period—the cadaverous Sal and fat Bessie—made a living by selling fish at Wooler. They have been immortalised in verse by the signalman at Beal, who must have seen the pair arguing and hawking fish from their cuds or donkeys on many occasions:

> Twas in that place called Holy Isle
> Two damsels dressed in fishwife style
> Each with a cud their way would wend
> Far up the country their fish to vend
> One was Sall—the other Bess
> The fish they hawked were seldom fresh
> But fresh or stale they aye got trade,
> By making dupes a living made.
> Sall was long and lean and lank
> Her shape was like a six foot plank
> Her mate, fat Bess, as her name implies
> Was a mass of flesh of enormous size

In the early part of the twentieth century, the large fishing-boat hulks were upturned on the beach by the Ouse and near the castle to act as storehouses, where they may still be seen today. These large boats were replaced by 25ft cobles or 33ft mules; these needed fewer crewmen and were used for line fishing and as lobster craft.

A brief respite for the white-fish trade followed World War I and catches increased; but within a few years they declined once more, and the 1920s and 1930s were the worst times the islanders had known for over a century. By the onset of World War II eight boats were fishing from the island and during the war only four cobles could be manned, although the price of fish was good.

In 1939 only 35 per cent of the diminished population of 243 was engaged in fishing; 13 per cent were farmers or labourers, and 15 per cent were in various trades or professions. For the first time the most common occupation, at 37 per cent, was in the holiday trade.

LAW AND ORDER

A village constable was responsible to the lord of the manor for law and order until the mid-nineteenth century, when, because of the numbers of transient visitors to the island, an officer of the Northumberland Constabulary was stationed there. About ten ships a month were calling at Lindisfarne in the 1880s and 1890s, usually coasting vessels passing through. To cater for the crews and fishermen there were at that time at least nine public houses on the island—the Ship Inn, Britannia, Fisherman's Arms, Selby Arms, Plough Inn, Iron Rails, Northumberland Arms, Castle Hotel and the Crown and Anchor.

Inn fights occurred frequently, but there is only one recorded incident of police intervention—this was a riot which took place on 22 February 1889. Hitherto law enforcement had been traditionally lax, but on this occasion, when a fisherman broke a window following a noisy gathering of inhabitants, a new and somewhat officious policeman, PC Johnston, nicknamed Joe Smoke, put the culprit in the lockup for the night. This incensed the islanders, who wrecked the police station, to the terror of the policeman's bed-ridden mother. The next day a contingent of mounted police came from the mainland to restore order. It is a measure of the feeling it generated that a petition was signed by almost all the inhabitants to have the constable removed. The vicar, the Reverend W. W. F. Keeling, a most popular man with the islanders, was amongst the signatories, but later withdrew his name under pressure from the lord of the manor.

The last constable to serve on the island was Henry Sanderson, who left in 1923.

The tidal races to the east of the island cause many ships to run on to the Farne Islands and rocks, or to go aground on the Goswick or Ross Sands. In addition there are many rocks around the island either awash at high water, such as the Plough, or dangerous at low water. The bar of Holy Island harbour has 8ft of water at low water, spring tide, but it is narrow and has shoals on either side. To the north there are the Burrows, Ploughseat and Willgate; to the south Partan Stiel and the Bat Shoal, and to the east the Goldstone, the Stiel and Guzzard Rocks. Light craft and fishing boats are in grave danger when they try and enter the harbour and there are heavy rolling breakers at the bar.

The safety of ships at sea was of great concern in the north-east in the early nineteenth century. Trinity House extended its powers over the Holy Island area by Act of Parliament in 1801. The beacon on Emanuel Head, erected in 1828, and other markers on the Plough Rock, the Heugh, in the fairways, and on the mainland south of the island are all maintained by Trinity House, to give safe access to and passage round the island.

The lifeboat service

The island's first lifeboat was built by Henry Greathead of South Shields in 1789 and donated by the Lord Crewe trustees. It was unnamed and little is known of its service record. This is true of the second lifeboat, built by Shone of Blackwall and also presented by the Lord Crewe trustees, which served the island from 1829 to 1864. These two early rowing boats were kept near the castle. The Institute of Shipwrecks, which later became the Royal National Lifeboat Institute, took over the management of the Holy Island station in 1865. A new lifeboat was given—a 32ft double-banked boat, named, appropriately, *Grace Darling*,

97

and a stone boat-house was built on the island close to St Cuthbert's Island.

Boats in distress on the sands south of the island were difficult to reach from the south-west corner of Holy Island as they were exposed to heavy broadside seas as they crossed the harbour. Because of this, a fishing boat had been used as a lifeboat from Ross Links for some years and in 1867 the Holy Island No 2 Station was set up on Ross Links with a new 32ft, ten-oared boat, the *Bombay*. This was crewed by island fishermen who sailed across the harbour in a light boat as the need arose. The Ross boat was difficult to launch on occasions because the boathouse was often exposed to the full force of the gale.

The Holy Island No 1 boat (*Grace Darling*) was at a disadvantage if a vessel was in distress to the north of the island at low water when the west passage along the Low was impassable. In 1891, the *Bombay* was replaced by the *Bedford*, a self-righting boat, which in turn was replaced, in 1900, by the *Edward and Eliza*, a pulling and sailing boat. Due to the few launchings from Ross and the other difficulties the No 2 Station was moved to the north side of the Snook in 1908, where it could serve the north and east of the island whatever the state of the tide.

The *Grace Darling* was replaced by a 34ft, ten-oared, self-righting vessel of the same name in 1884. This was replaced in 1910 by the *Lizzie Porter*, a 35ft pulling and sailing boat with two drop keels. In 1925 came the *Milburn*, the island's first motor lifeboat, a 45ft Watson cabin type and only the third to be stationed in Northumberland at the time. A new lifeboat house to the south of the Heugh, with a ramp into the harbour, was built to accommodate this vessel. The increased efficiency of the *Milburn* resulted in the closure of the Snook Station in March 1934. The *Gertrude* replaced the *Milburn* in 1946.

Lifeboat services were withdrawn from the island in 1968, following the report of a working party of the RNLI Management Committee on the most efficient deployment of lifeboats.

Shipping is in less danger nowadays because of modern navigational aids and lifeboats are more powerful, so that the same cover can be achieved with less expense for the RNLI. The departure of the lifeboats was deeply regretted, not only because the station was one of the earliest in Britain, but because of the record of successes the island boats achieved. Since 1865, 205 launches were made and 336 lives saved. Fifteen medals were awarded to island crew members—one gold and four silver before 1865 and eight silver and two bronze since then. No lives were ever lost from the crews of rescue boats, although a man was once washed overboard in 1937 and rescued, and on one memorable occasion the *Milburn* and its entire crew turned turtle in the harbour and righted itself with all hands safe.

Outstanding rescues

One of the major difficulties with the early boats was to get them launched into a head wind. A horse could not always be used and the boat, weighing 2–3 tons, had then to be pushed into the sea by the islanders. One such occasion was on Sunday, 15 January 1922, during a south-easterly gale and a blinding snow storm. The *James B. Graham*, a trawler from Hartlepool, was on the rocks off Emanuel Head. It was low tide and the carriage wheels of the *Lizzie Porter* sank deep into the mud. The boat was launched with great difficulty by sixty villagers, twenty-five of them women, all of whom had to wade waist-deep into the sea. The rescue proved a most dangerous and time-consuming operation for which a silver clasp and two bronze medals were awarded.

Coxswain George Cromarty, who received the clasp, had earned his silver medal six years before for his part in the rescue of the crew from the *Jolani*, a Norwegian barque. In a hurricane on 19 November 1916, it was seen drifting north past Emanuel Head and towards Goswick Sands. The No 2 boat was called out at 2.40pm. By the time the men and horses got to the boathouse, the ship was further north and the lifeboat had to be transported on its carriage six miles along the shore, the men wading knee deep in water. When they eventually reached the wrecked ship, only the stern remained, with fourteen men on it. The lifeboat had still to be launched, but the east-south-east hurricane and tremendous seas flung it back to the shore time after time, as attempts were made to get under way. The boat finally got away, although it proved impossible to get near the wreck owing to floating debris. The lifeboatmen were exhausted, but returned to the wreck an hour later when the tide turned. They could not get alongside, but by midnight the coxswain managed to get a line on board and the fourteen men were saved.

Often fishermen were out at sea when help was required and scratch crews had to be assembled. On 2 February 1892, the vicar, W. W. F. Keeling, took out the lifeboat in the absence of the regular coxswain. The next vicar, the Reverend Bryson, had a similar experience. All the fishing boats were out when the sea rose unexpectedly, making crossing the bar hazardous. He raised a crew which included the sexton, a fish merchant and some sick sailors, and the women launched the lifeboat. The fishing boats were safely escorted into the harbour.

Salvage

Many vessels went aground during the two world wars and a variety of strange objects were washed ashore, all valuable salvage: lead pencils, Chinese bank notes, ping pong balls, phials of drugs, cabbages, whisky, candles, pit props, cigarettes and coal.

Grounded ships were a much more valuable prize. The *Prins Knud*, a 2,000-ton Danish vessel, ran aground to the north of the island in 1940. It took six weeks of hard labour by the entire population for a channel to be dug and the ship refloated; for their efforts, the islanders received £3,200 in salvage dues.

In the fierce winter of 1947, the roads to the island were blocked by snow for nearly a week and provisions were getting low. On 15 March, the *Gertrude* was launched to fetch supplies from Berwick and also the body of a man who was to be buried on the island the next day.

The final links with the RNLI were severed in 1970 when the launching station, not an object of beauty, under the Heugh, was demolished. All that now remains of the lifeboats on Holy Island are the earlier lifeboat houses on the Snook and by Hob Thrush, the records of rescues on the wall by the museum, and the memories of a dwindling number of island inhabitants.

6   LIFE ON LINDISFARNE TODAY

THE occupants of the island have gradually changed in type as well as in person; nowadays there are three clear categories of islanders. Firstly there are the residents who, like their ancestors, were born and bred on the island and have many family connections there. This is the inner or core group of islanders, some of whom can trace their ancestry back to medieval villagers. In 1970 there were seventy-one males and fifty-seven females in this category. The second group comprises those, mainly women, who have married into the core group and come to live on the island; there were forty-six of them in 1970. The final group number thirty or so transient inhabitants who have no long-term associations with the island —some are in employment; others in retirement, and some are the owners of holiday houses and only live on the island intermittently. Several of the core community leave the island for long holidays during the winter months.

For all these reasons, it is difficult to count the total number of inhabitants; in 1970 it varied between 190 and 210, a preponderance of the inhabitants being over the age of fifty. There were none between the ages of forty-five and forty-nine, and only one girl in the age group between fifteen and nineteen. The community therefore consisted of three distinct generations, the younger the group the smaller its size.

This unusual situation arose because of the number of islanders who left during the 1920s and 1930s; they brought up families on the mainland and often retired to the island, but without their grown-up children. In recent years more young

Page 103 (above) A Roman Catholic pilgrimage of the 1950s. The party is assembling at Chare Ends, some having walked across the sands; *(below)* the royal visit of 1958. The Queen and the Duke of Edinburgh meet Miss Kate Parbury by her sculpture of St Aidan, in the churchyard

Page 104 Holy Island priory church: *(above left)* part of the shaft of an eighth-century and *(above right)* a ninth-century free-standing cross found in the ruins; *(below)* the arcade of the north nave shows a sculptured column similar to those in Durham Cathedral. The west front shows the large processional door and the later fortifications added above the old church roof

couples have stayed on the island because of the better economic prospects and the availability of houses. This has resulted in more births on the island; thirty-two over the last decade—a hopeful sign that the core community will not disappear, although it is unlikely to return to the size it was in the nineteenth century.

ISLAND TRADITIONS

Many old Northumbrian customs have lingered on in Holy Island when they have been lost elsewhere. Nick (tee) names are still continually and preferentially used on the island. Those in modern usage include: Poppy, Crow, Lulu, Wonker, Bones, Farmer, Slim, Tam, Bim, Dancer, Rufus, Coolie, Buck, Tinko, Tar, Bobo and Bucken. These are often acquired in early childhood and kept throughout the life of an individual, some being passed on to that person's offspring. This is just the way some surnames were acquired in medieval times.

The Holy Island dialect is peculiar to the village; it has been studied by linguists from Switzerland and dialectologists from Scotland. Some aspects of it fit into a category characteristic of the east coast of Scotland, the most southerly part of this dialect group being found between Berwick and Holy Island. For example, the words used in relation to small-line fishing have been investigated and shown to fit into the type of pattern found in the Scottish fishing ports south of Fife.

There is a wide variety of local names for wild life, some of which are still in use: 'crow fish' for spiny crab; dead man's grief (sea campion); bell duck (coot); watery (wagtail); St Cuthbert's ducks (eiders) and St Cuthbert's beads (crinoid fossils). St Cuthbert is the best remembered island saint and many early lives recall his love of the local birdlife. The crinoids, the fossil stems of Carboniferous water creatures, can be found off the west coast of the island.

Bridal garlands are no longer hung in the church after a wedding ceremony—those which Dr George Johnston saw when he visited the island in 1854 were from weddings long before—but other marriage customs are still in existence. The bride has to jump the 'petting stone' supported by two old fishermen or the two oldest male inhabitants. The stone is situated between the chancel of St Mary's church and the priory and is, in fact, the base stone of a pre-Norman free-standing cross. A clear jump signifies good fortune and fertility in the marriage. Newly married couples are greeted by islanders firing shot guns. The church gates are tied and a 'fine' has to be distributed to pass through. Another custom involves breaking plates by throwing them over the head of the bride, a broken plate being a lucky sign.

At a funeral, a farmer acts as undertaker and heads the procession from the deceased's residence to meet the vicar at the churchyard gate. The undertaker, wearing a black tail coat and tall hat, precedes the coffin which is carried by six islanders. If it is the funeral of a well-known inhabitant, the entire village will attend, walking behind the coffin. The island women walk together, many carrying flowers, and the men bring up the rear wearing their usual costume of blue sweaters, cloth caps and raincoats. The procession can be very long but is usually eerily silent, in direct contrast to a wedding ceremony.

On the Saturday night before the fourth Sunday in Lent, the inns provide carlings, which are dried peas, taken with rum and sugar. The adult men at one time had a mumming type ceremony on Easter Monday called paste-egging. The Sundays during Lent and Easter are recalled by the rhyme:

> Tid, Mid, Miserae
> Carling, Palm, Paste Egg Day.

Fishermen accumulate traditions, of which there are several on the island. Only fishermen may sit in the north aisle, or Haggerston aisle, of the church; their wives and children sit in the central aisle. Fishermen are typically superstitious on a number of topics: they will not willingly fish with women or clergymen in the boat, and some would not even put out to fish if they saw a nun or a cross-eyed woman that morning. The word 'pig' is of particular significance; no fisherman will say it and the entire island considers it to be a most unlucky word. In the days when women baited the lines, if they saw a pig whilst doing this or spoke the word, they considered the line incapable of catching fish and would start again. These superstitions do not prevent the islanders from eating pork or keeping pigs on the island. Pigs are, however, always referred to as 'yon things' or 'articles' or 'grumfits'.

EMPLOYMENT

The non-islanders employed on the island include the vicar, the district nurse, the management of the mead works, a publican, the postmistress, the priory guide and the schoolmistress. Few of the true islanders have single occupations; variations occur seasonally and with the time of day. A farmer, for example, may help with a guesthouse in the summer, and a man who fishes in the morning may deliver coal in the afternoon. The major occupations of the core islanders are now fishing, farming, hotel and guesthouse keeping, trades and services.

Nowadays a maximum of ten people are concerned with farming, that is about 16 per cent of the adult core population. There is one large farm of about 400 acres and a smaller concern of 30–40 acres. The farms rent some land from the church and the National Trust. Much of the land is used for grazing sheep and raising beef cattle; a few fields are set aside for hay and wheat, and there are some acres of arable near Chare Ends. In the late 1960s a small pig-fattening concern was set up near the priory.

About sixteen men, or 27 per cent of the adult population, are employed in the five fishing boats, and three or four people occasionally help with the gathering and preparation of mussels and winkles. In March all five boats fish for crab and lobster; catches are poor until the summer with a peak in the early autumn. Three of the boats hold licences to fish for salmon and trout. Salmon fishing, by drift nets, usually starts in June and lasts until August. White fish are caught fitfully, as the conditions merit, often whilst drift netting. All five boats are fishing for lobster once more in September. November and December are the closed season for crab fishing. In addition to the old hulks which serve as huts for tackle, there are sheds sheltering under the Heugh. A small extension to the landing stage at Steel End facilitates loading and unloading the boats.

About fourteen island families are directly involved with the holiday trade—which includes private hotels and guesthouses, public houses, four small shops only open in summer, and holiday cottages. Islanders run the old post office and the general store, and help in the museum. Others are employed by the mead works, in some taxi work, in the odd boat trip to the Farnes, or in wildfowling with boats or punts. Up to 65 per cent of the population can be involved in these activities.

Islanders also deliver mail, look after the water system, clear the coast road of debris, carry coal and fish and act as part-time coastguards and members of the emergency rocket team. A few islanders work on the mainland, in Newcastle and elsewhere, and return to the island at weekends.

The council workman who attends to the roads and the water tower lives on the island. Other services, including the refuse collectors, come from the mainland.

SERVICES

Lindisfarne is now a part of Berwick District Council, the island representative being appropriately the present lord of the manor. The parish council is the smallest local authority unit in Britain to have a coat of arms. It was given by the Northumberland Motor Club in June 1959 and shows a monk holding the

Lindisfarne Gospels, the crown of St Oswald and St Cuthbert's cross.

Social and medical services

There is an excess of old people in the permanently resident group; about half the population—against a national average of only 16·5 per cent—is over sixty-five years of age. This is reflected by the number of referals made to the Northumberland County Council Social Services Department. Five requests were made during 1973 for help with problems on the island—that is one request per 38 of the population compared to the mainland average of one request per 100 inhabitants.

The nearest medical practice is in Belford, 10½ miles from the village. This is a dispensing practice and medicines are brought to the district nurse on the island. She looks after the islanders' day-to-day needs and liaises with the practice in Belford. The villagers may have to attend hospital clinics at Berwick, Ashington or Newcastle. Antenatal care is undertaken at Berwick; some births take place there, at Alnwick or on the island. No clinics exist on Lindisfarne, but it is hoped to start a mother and baby class soon. The islanders usually visit dentists or opticians in Berwick upon Tweed.

A home help service is provided by a mainland woman, when requested by the district nurse. A meals service for old people has been integrated into the school meals facility. A representative of the social services visits the island regularly.

Education

The village school is a one-teacher Church of England School under the authority of the Northumberland Education Committee. In 1975 it became a First School taking pupils from five to nine years of age, the older children boarding at Tweedmouth, where those over the age of eleven have, since 1966, been weekly boarders.

The late-eighteenth-century building housing the village

109

school has been improved in recent years and comprises two classrooms, a kitchen and cloakrooms, with an adjoining residence for the teacher. The number of pupils has dwindled over the past twenty years:

1955	23	1960	13	1965	12	1970	9
1956	22	1961	9	1966	10	1971	10
1957	21	1962	10	1967	8	1972	14
1958	14	1963	9	1968	9	1973	14
1959	15	1964	9	1969	9		

This decline is partly due to the departure of young families from the island for economic reasons, and partly to the change from an all-age school to a primary school.

School meals are cooked on the premises by a cook and there is one meals assistant. A part-time caretaker is responsible for the running of the school.

Housing

Housing is a topic of major concern on the island; the tourist boom has meant that young couples would like to stay if they could find proper housing. In common with other beautiful, rural areas in Britain, the island has seen property increase greatly in value and many outsiders have acquired houses or land. Houses which have passed to relatives living on the mainland are often used by them as holiday cottages. Land has been bought occasionally for building houses or bungalows for new permanent residents. In recent years the old herring houses by the Ouse have been converted and some houses in Fenkle Street, Marygate and Fiddler's Green rebuilt. A row of three houses, built near the Iron Rails Inn to accommodate the island's coastguards, have now passed to the Department of the Environment guides. In 1972 nine council dwellings were built on the site of the stockyards in the centre of the village, four being three-bedroomed houses and the rest two-bedroomed bungalows; there are also eight garages on the site. This new property fits in neatly with the rest of the village.

Water supply

Piped water came to the island in 1955, prior to this all the water had to be pumped manually from shallow wells; the most popular was the Popple Well near the Iron Rails. The new water system consists of a borehole and a water tower just above Lewins Lane which has a licence not to exceed 24,000 gallons a day. In 1960 a modern sewerage system was installed which consists of maceration followed by marine discharge at Castle Point immediately after each high water. Public toilets have been built near the village hall and by the car park.

Electricity

In 1957 electricity was brought to the island by the South of Scotland Electricity Board. Overhead cables brought the grid to Beal and then the cable was laid under the sand by the aid of a mole plough. At Chare Ends the cables are taken overhead to supply the entire island by a series of sub-stations, including one at the castle and one for the pump at the water borehole. A limited number of street lights were introduced in 1970.

Rescue services

The rescue services are an important aspect, extensively used by permanent residents and visitors alike. Between 1971 and 1973, the Berwick Ambulance Station took 104 emergency cases off the island, about twenty of which were extremely urgent. There was one emergency for every two permanent residents. If an emergency occurs when the tide is up, the patient has to remain on the island until an ambulance can get through, or be taken to Beal by boat, punt or high-bodied lorry. An RAF helicopter was used on 25 May 1970 to take a five-week-old baby to hospital in Newcastle.

Fire engines, which come from Morpeth since local stations

were closed in 1948, have been delayed in the past by the tide, fortunately without serious consequences. Because of the possibility of delay, there is a volunteer fire party on the island, with equipment to tap the main water supply; there are twelve fire hydrants in the village. The Nature Conservancy Council also provides beaters for dealing with grass fires.

Car accidents and strandings on the causeway are frequent, despite tide tables and warning notices. A telephone in the refuge box can be used to alert the police, who organise the rescue. This usually entails waiting until the tide goes down and arranging for the local garage at Beal to restart the engine of the stranded vehicle. Only rarely do the inshore rescue boat, lifeboat or helicopter have to be brought in to rescue people from the refuge box. Between 1967 and 1971 an RAF helicopter was called out seven times to take people off the causeway. Over the last four years, several fatal accidents have occurred on the road and fifteen people have had to be taken off various sand spits in the area.

AMENITIES

Life on Lindisfarne is more like that of an isolated village than that of an island. The amenities available to the islanders have greatly increased over the last three decades. A bus service now operates twice a week to Berwick, while many islanders own cars and are in the habit of giving lifts to the mainland. A few of the older inhabitants, who rarely leave the island, are able to buy all they require there. Two general stores are open all the year round, one of which acts as a newsagents. Daily supplies are obtained from a variety of mobile delivery vehicles, mostly from Berwick. These include a milkman (every day in summer, alternate days in winter); greengrocers (three different suppliers); two butchers (one twice a week and the other three times); two bakers (three times a week); fishmonger (twice a week); laundryman (once a week), and icecream vans in summer. Weekly shopping is almost always carried out in Berwick upon Tweed and special shopping in Newcastle.

Telephones

The first telephone was connected in 1893 when a cable was laid across the sands. The first public call box was installed in 1926 when a new cable was laid, and the following year a small manual exchange was opened with two lines direct to Berwick upon Tweed. This was replaced by a small automatic exchange on Chare Ends Road. A new exchange is to provide subscriber trunk dialling facilities and more lines to the island, while the overhead telephone lines are gradually being placed underground.

Leisure

Leisure time on the island differs little from that in other Northumbrian fishing villages. The Anglican church and the school are the centres for group activities which in recent years have included drama classes, resulting in a popular village show; the making of a carpet for the church; an Easter play for children in the church, and an evening keep-fit class for ladies. There are regular whist drives, male and female darts teams, and two annual events which have been taking place for many years—the Christmas party and the yachtsmen's supper.

Many islanders actively support Newcastle United Football Club. There are still a few pigeon fanciers on the island; some islanders keep allotments, and others are amateur naturalists. Wildfowling—a sport, pastime and occupation rolled into one—is an interest shared by many visitors to the island.

The children enjoy the rural freedom of their island existence, although they do occasionally regret their meagre numbers when it comes to football and other team games. There are piano lessons available for them, as well as a dancing class.

The media

An important aspect of island life is the amount of attention given to it by newspapers and the television companies. In the last few years ITV programmes about the island have included *Holy Island—The other Lindisfarne*, shown in March 1972; *About Britain—The Northumberland Coast*, in November 1972, and *An Island twice a day* in January 1973. There were three similar features on BBC television during the same period. Holy Island and its nearby sands have been a venue for television plays, including *Cul-de-Sac* starring Donald Pleasance, and for such major films as *Macbeth*, directed by Roman Polanski.

Poets, novelists and artists have used Holy Island as a setting for their work for many years. More recently it has been featured by Frank Graham in a children's story and by Lorna Hill in her novel, *Five Shilling Holiday*. Gordon Honeycombe's novel, *Dragon under the Hill*, is vividly set in the present-day village. The northern pop group, Lindisfarne, based part of their publicity schemes on the island.

7   TOURISM

ALTHOUGH the island is geographically isolated, at no time in its history has there been any lack of visitors. In medieval times there were pilgrims to the shrines of the saints; refugees from the Scottish wars; shipwrecked seamen, and mainlanders with property on the island, as well as those with business at the priory. Soldiers, coastguards, customs men, labourers, merchants and salesmen added to the diversity of island visitors. One group and then another gradually declined on the island, only to be replaced by another phenomenon—the idly curious. With the increase in leisure time and the changes in the nature of English society, these people greatly increased in numbers to become the tourists of the late nineteenth and twentieth centuries.

Tourism proper started in the late eighteenth century; Hutchinson says of the island in 1794 that 'it is of late years becoming a place of great resort'. Then, as today, people went there for health and relaxation, while others were attracted to the island for botanical, ornithological, sporting and historical reasons.

The tourist trade was greatly facilitated by a series of guides and other books about the island. The earliest guide and history was written by the Reverend W. W. F. Keeling in the 1880s. Holy Island as a health resort received a boost in 1883 from the publication by Dr Ellis of his *Medical Guide to Health Resorts*. He suggested bathing from Sandon Bay, as well as recommending the island to give relief for many types of illness, debility, depression and sleeplessness.

PILGRIMS

Pilgrims were among the earliest visitors to the island, and they still come in large numbers, often in organised groups. There are references to a revival of the early pilgrimages taking place in the nineteenth century. One series of Roman Catholic pilgrimages were organised by Canon Consett, a regular visitor to the island for many years. Since then hardly a year passes without several, either Roman Catholic or Anglican, being organised; often booklets are produced to mark the occasion. In 1951, for example, a pilgrimage booklet, *St Aidan of Lindisfarne,* was specially written by Father Wilson, the priest in charge at Buckworth, to mark the 1,3000th anniversary of the death of St Aidan. In 1958, the Reverend James W. Kennedy, an American Episcopalian, published *Holy Island, a Lenten Pilgrimage,* as a result of a personal pilgrimage to the island the previous year. Among recent pilgrims there have been two Archbishops of York, many bishops and numerous other clergy, both Anglican and Roman Catholic. All these pilgrims make a valuable contribution to the quality of life on the island, as well as renewing and reinforcing its religious significance.

ROYAL VISITORS

On 2 July 1908 the Prince and Princess of Wales visited Holy Island during their stay with the Duke of Northumberland at Alnwick Castle. A bouquet was presented to them by the island children and a basket decorated with shells by the adults. The royal couple then planted two sycamore trees in the garden of the Manor House—now the hotel—and also visited the castle and priory.

Between that royal visit and another fifty years later, the old style Holy Island disappeared and the present age of tourism began. The second royal visit was initiated by the vicar, the Reverend T. J. Martin; £30,000 was required to renovate the church so he founded an appeal committee under royal patronage. In 1958 the whole plan came to fruition. When the Queen and the Duke of Edinburgh visited the island on St Peter's Day, 29 June, it was the first occasion for over a thousand years that a reigning monarch had visited Holy Island. Having attended morning service and met several islanders, the Queen visited the priory ruins and the castle. She and the Duke planted trees in the square and received as parting gifts a shell basket (a local craft revived by the tourist trade) and twenty-eight lobsters. The appeal for the church repair fund was launched the next day and, thanks to the additional publicity, was very successful. The royal visit may also have stimulated public interest in the island, since the enormous increase in day visitors dates from that time.

TOURIST FACILITIES

Access

In the early nineteenth century, the most direct route to the village over the sands was marked by 270 poles, many of which can still be seen on the old Pilgrims' Way, where two refuge boxes were also placed to serve a similar purpose to the present box on the causeway. A further hundred poles indicated the route across the South Low which is now followed by the metalled road.

The construction of this road was the most important factor in stimulating tourist traffic to the island. Short experimental sections of metalled roadway were built on the Beal side of the sands in 1929 and 1949. The consistency of the sand was good and the tide had little effect on the surface. With this assurance, a further 1,420 yards were constructed in 1954, connecting the Beal Road with the Snook; this included the 50 yard-long bridge across the Low. The next part of the road, the 2 mile stretch between the Snook and Chare Ends, was completed in 1966 at a cost of £36,000.

The road needs surprisingly little maintenance; it has to be cleared of seaweed and debris quite regularly and the groynes near the Low have to be repaired and a new surface dressing put down every three years. In 1969 the road to the east of the bridge was lifted and turning bays made. The road means that access to the island by car is much safer and easier and the chassis does not get a soaking in salt water. The tides still cover the bridge with 1–7ft of water; tide tables and times of safe passage are clearly marked at several points on the road and in the village.

The increasing use of the road is shown dramatically by three traffic censuses made on the Beal Road: the first, from 5 to 11 May 1954, about the time the causeway was opened, recorded 174 vehicles in both directions, of which 168 were the old island taxis—the new road put an end to this type of transport. Over three days in May 1968, 680 vehicles crossed to the island, and during five days in August 1972 13,040 vehicles passed the census point—an enormous number for such a small island. A large car park was constructed in 1958 through the generosity of Mr T. Clark, of Seaham Harbour.

Accommodation

The many inns and taverns of the nineteenth century had dwindled by 1908 to the four which exist today, but there was a gradual increase in holiday accommodation on the island. By 1950 there were three private hotels, thirteen boarding houses, and at least five cottages which took in occasional guests, also a café and three small shops. Relatively few visitors are accommodated on the island even today, however, and tents and caravans are not allowed.

Amenities

In 1907 a nine-hole golf course was laid out on the Links by James Braid, but this has now closed down. The island also became a popular harbour for yachtsmen, with an annual regatta held by the Northumberland Yacht Club. By 1939 there was a fleet of eleven taxicabs on the island; while a village hall, provided by Mr E. de Stein, had been opened on 14 August 1931. Islanders and visitors alike enjoyed the billiards and other facilities of the hall, as well as those of the library and reading room.

The enormous numbers of day visitors attracted to the island have brought renewed prosperity in recent years; each day-tripper spends only a little money and stays only a few hours, visiting certain parts of the island, but the cumulative effect is considerable, and the flow of tourists has been quite unaffected by the closure, in 1968, of the nearest railway station, at Beal.

TOURIST ATTRACTIONS

Some estimates, based on the number of coaches coming to the island, suggest that in 1970 the number of visitors was about 100,000 and in 1973 over 200,000. Most tourists visit only part of the island—the village, the Ouse, the castle, the ruins of the priory, and the parish church. The numbers inspecting the castle and priory are given below:

	Priory	*Castle*
1962	24,700	—
1963	20,400	2,044
1964	20,700	2,330
1965	19,000	4,438
1966	19,600	5,606
1967	27,700	6,370
1968	32,800	8,810
1969	29,700	20,455
1970	41,000	20,694
1971	53,000	21,561
1972	55,400	19,398*
1973	—	32,696

*excluding members of the National Trust

THE HOLY ISLAND OF LINDISFARNE

In 1971 Holy Island Priory was the seventh most popular tourist site in Northumberland and Durham. The castle is probably relatively as popular, but is only open in the summer. Many items of archaeological and historical interest, excavated from the priory ruins, were collected and put in an outhouse of the old Manor House. Since the Department of Works took over the priory site, this has become a small museum, administered along with the priory and separate from the Manor House Hotel; the museum, by the churchyard gates, can be visited when the ruins are open.

The limekilns by the castle have recently been included in the Department of the Environment's list of buildings of particular interest and the National Trust is in the process of repairing them.

In the village, interest centres around the small shops in the Square and Marygate. Also popular with visitors is the Mead Factory where the Lindisfarne Liqueur Company, founded in 1962, produces mead and a liqueur which is a blend of two single malt whiskies with honey and herbs. It also markets a fudge and a marmalade which contain a certain proportion of the liqueur. The products are sold all over the world and no doubt attract curious travellers to the island from very far afield. The showrooms also provide café facilities for tourists and employment for a few island women. The small partly prefabricated factory, store and showrooms, known as St Aidan's Winery, are near the Presbyterian Church. The company has been recently awarded a grant from the Industrial Development Board.

THE VISITOR'S GUIDE TO HOLY ISLAND

How to get there

By car, travel on the A1 road through Northumberland—north from Alnwick or south from Berwick upon Tweed. The Beal road turning to the east is clearly signposted near an inn and petrol station, and leads directly to the island.

By rail, travel to Berwick upon Tweed and take a local bus to Beal lane end; or, on Saturdays and Wednesdays, a new service (477) which goes direct to the island at times depending on the tides.

Crossing to the island

Crossings must be made two hours before or three and a half hours after a high tide. Tide tables may be obtained for the year from The Old Post Office, Holy Island, Berwick upon Tweed (telephone: Holy Island 241). The tables may be seen in local information centres throughout the north and in the northern daily papers. Weekly tide tables are displayed on the Beal road; on either side of the causeway bridge; on the road to Chare Ends, and in the village square. If in doubt do not attempt to cross; the tide can be very deceptive.

If in difficulty on the causeway when crossing by car, leave the vehicle at once and climb into the refuge box, where further instructions are given. When crossing to the island on foot, exercise great caution and allow much longer than the anticipated crossing time so as to be safe in case of a mishap. It is over four miles to Holy Island village from Beal lane end.

Where to stay

There is a choice of inns, small guesthouses and private hotels listed by the AA and RAC: the Lindisfarne, Manor House, Bamburgh View, Farne View, Britannia House, Links View and Castle View. In addition, there is Marygate House, the Christian Centre guesthouse in Marygate. There are a few cottages to let; inquiries can be made at the Iron Rails Inn.

What to see

The priory, and the nearby museum, are open on weekdays all the year round and an entrance fee is charged:

H

March–April	9.30am–5.30pm
May–September	9.30am–7pm
October	9.30am–3.30pm
November–February	9.30am–4pm

In the winter months the priory and museum close at midday for the lunch hour.

The castle is open daily (except Tuesdays) from 2pm to 6pm between March 31 and June 3 and between June 21 and September 30. The limekilns and castle garden are also open at stated times.

Other places to visit

The south part of the island is easy to reach on foot; cars can be left in the car park to the north of the village. When walking on the sand dunes visitors are asked to take care not to damage the soil and not to pick any plants. Places notable for the views are the Ouse, the Heugh, St Cuthbert's Island, Castle Point, the east coast and Emanuel Head. The village itself is well worth a close inspection. In the churchyard there is a large bronze sculpture of St Aidan by Miss Kate Parbury, until recently an island resident, and unveiled when the Queen visited the island in 1958. In the summer months the vicar is often in the church and will help those interested in the church and its work on the island.

Church services

Sunday services at the parish church are as follows: Holy Communion 8am; Parish Communion 10.30am; Evensong 6pm.

Services are held at the Presbyterian church on alternate Sundays at 6pm.

The Roman Catholic Chapel has services throughout the summer months.

Postal services

There are two collections from Monday to Friday at 11.30am

and 5.15pm and one, at 11.30am, on Saturday. This does not mean the letters are taken to Berwick upon Tweed at these times; that depends on the daily state of the tides. The sub-post office near the Market Square is open 9am–1pm and 2pm–5.30pm on weekdays, and from 9am to 12 noon on Saturdays.

8   THE FUTURE OF HOLY ISLAND

MANY islanders and visitors, who knew the island before the changes brought about by the growth of tourism during the 1950s and 1960s, bitterly regret the present situation and regard the future with deep foreboding. They fear that further development may utterly destroy what remains of the character of the island. There are others, however, who would like an extension of tourist amenities—a caravan park, amusement centres, cafés and so on— which would greatly increase the prosperity of the island. Outside planners, the Nature Conservancy Council and other authorities have their own opinions on the consequences of over-development and exploitation.

The island is thus facing a controversial future and the inhabitants, especially the core community, are caught in a situation they feel to be beyond their control. There are some indications, however, that Lindisfarne will be able to retain its character and at the same time add to its prosperity.

OVERALL PLANNING

The entire North Northumberland coast, including Holy Island, is designated as an Area of Outstanding Natural Beauty; this means that official restraints can be applied to projects which would harm the future appreciation of the area. The coast and Holy Island have also been made into a Heritage Coast, which gives added powers to local authorities. Control of planning activities is in the hands of the district councils, which deal with matters within existing policy; whilst the North-umberland County Council oversees these decisions and deals with other matters outside.

Because of the many restrictions placed on Holy Island by the government and other bodies, there is to be effectively no development, except what is needed for the essential require-ments of the island inhabitants. The following would therefore be allowed: small industrial developments or extensions in the village; infilling in the village, and the purchase and renovation of second homes; council houses, and a second car park if a site could be found. All new developments or alterations must be of a very high standard of design and in keeping with the rest of the village. Caravans and unfitting tourist developments will not be allowed. In practice, there are very few applications for development; so much of this has not been put to the test. Nevertheless, it seems there is little risk of the village becoming a tourist 'nightmare'.

LOCAL TRENDS

The island population

The indications are that the population structure will con-tinue to change over the next two decades. The present older group will decline in numbers, and the smaller middle group will be filled out by mainlanders. At present the younger generation is increasing and it is this group which will largely determine the island's future. Young people will be more likely to stay on the island if housing remains available at reasonable rates and the economic outlook is fair. The return of prosperous fishing could mean another boom for the island if it were ex-ploited to the full. Other schemes, such as mussel breeding or lug-worm catching, could supplement the present inshore fish-ing and provide more jobs for young people. The island would be a much more stable place if it had a major additional source of income besides tourism.

THE HOLY ISLAND OF LINDISFARNE

Conservation

One outside body with particular interests in Holy Island is the Nature Conservancy Council. It would prefer a policy of relatively slow change and preservation rather than any rapid exploitation of the south of the island, which would inevitably attract many more people to the sand dunes. Even the comparatively few people who currently visit the nature reserve are quite unwittingly causing erosion of the dunes, with a consequent risk that a large part of the island will be blown away. It is for this reason that the Nature Conservancy Council is opposed to the National Trust establishing a tourist information centre at Beal, which could create an increase in traffic to the island and a greater number of people frequenting the dunes. Methods of stabilising and preserving the dunes and their unique flora will undoubtedly continue, but over the years the entire area may have to be fenced off, in portions, to achieve stability.

Place of pilgrimage

According to the Oxford English Dictionary the word 'pilgrim' means one 'who travels from place to place' and also one 'who visits places as acts of religious devotion'. If Holy Island is to remain worthy of pilgrims, in both senses of the word, any changes must be for the benefit of the islanders, while its attraction for the visitor must also play a major part in planning for the future. But there must be none of the synthetic 'tourist fishing village' about it. It should be a naturally developing and well cared for area, with modern life manifestly continuing around its historical sites. To this end, a careful course will need to be followed in order to maintain it as a living and attractive place of pilgrimage. For, even in the rich variety of the British heritage, the ancient and holy island of Lindisfarne can justly claim to be unique.

9   THE FARNE ISLANDS

THE Farne Islands lie six to seven miles to the south and east of Holy Island, a few miles offshore from Bamburgh and Seahouses. These islands have already been mentioned as the retreat of St Cuthbert and as the breeding ground of many of the sea-birds and seals seen near Holy Island. For these reasons this brief guide to what may be seen on the Farnes is included.

How to get there

Although some Holy Island fishermen will occasionally take visitors directly to the Farne Islands, the usual and shorter route, of about a mile, to Inner Farne, is to embark from Seahouses. Regular trips are available during the holiday season, run by several local fishermen, and, peak holiday periods apart, there is usually ample room in the boats. Some trips are scheduled by bus and coach companies each season and special excursions are organised by natural history societies. Advance booking is recommended, as some islands have restricted visiting, and any enquiries should first be made of The Warden, The Sheiling, 8 St Aidan's, Seahouses, Northumberland (Seahouses (066 572) 651). The times of trips vary with the tides and local weather conditions—the journey can be very rough—and the cost is about £1 per adult, in addition to a landing fee. Reductions are made for parties and members of the National Trust. More detailed information is available from tourist information centres in the north-east of England.

THE FARNE ISLANDS

There are 28 islands in the Farne group, many of which are covered by the tide whilst others are simply bare rocks. The largest is Inner Farne, nearest to the mainland, which is 16 acres in area at low water. Beyond Inner Farne lie the two Wideopens, while the rest of the major islands lie further out to sea to the north-east, beyond the mile-wide channel of Staples Sound. These include Staple Island and Brownsman, and further north the Wamses, the Harcars and Longstone.

Most boat trips include a run round all the larger islands and this offers a good opportunity to observe their geology. The islands are peaks of hard, dolerite rock which has weathered above water into magnificent cliffs and sea-stacks. In particular, the Pinnacles to the south of Staples and the 6oft high Stack Rock near Inner Farne are worthy of note. Equally spectacular is the sea at the Churn, to the west of Inner Farne, when a storm is rising. Here the water comes up a short channel and rises through a blow hole in an enormous spout, up to 100ft.

The islands themselves are bare of trees, only a few having acquired enough soil for any vegetation. The soil itself—based on boulder clay and accumulated bird droppings—is unique in a temperate climate. There are freshwater springs and the site of an old well on Inner Farne, but the other islands are without fresh water.

The group has been described in medieval documents and was mapped by Speed in the seventeenth century, since when the islands seem to have changed very little.

HISTORY

Most of the historical sites are on Inner Farne, the place of Cuthbert's isolation. No remains now exist of Anglo-Saxon work here, with the possible exception of a well under Prior

Castell's tower. This is a pele tower, built about 1500 by a prior of Durham, and the traditional site of St Cuthbert's cell. Durham erected a medieval priory on the island, with a guest house and two chapels. Some ruins beyond the tower are the remains of the guest house, named as a 'Fishe-house' on Speed's map. One chapel, dedicated to St Mary, has now disappeared while the other, St Cuthbert's, built in 1370, was restored by Archdeacon Thorpe in 1848. This man, who later purchased the island from the Dean and Chapter of Durham, also added some seventeenth-century woodwork brought from Durham Cathedral. Parts of the medieval chapel can be picked out in the rebuilt church.

During the late sixteenth and early seventeenth centuries the island was garrisoned, using the pele as a fortress. Later, in the seventeenth century, the tower acted as the first lighthouse, burning coal in a brazier each night. A modern oil-burning lighthouse was built in 1809, and this was eventually replaced by an automatic acetylene light which is still there today. All the islands were bought for the National Trust in 1925, and in recent years the only inhabitants have been the wardens of the nature reserve and various scientists making use of the facilities on Inner Farne.

The other islands have little of great antiquity associated with them. The Staples and Brownsman have the remains of lighthouses, and the most isolated island, Longstone, has a functioning, manned lighthouse, first built in 1826. The erection of this light made the Brownsman light redundant and its keeper, William Darling, was moved to the new Longstone light. It was from here that he and his daughter, Grace, rescued survivors from the *Forfarshire* which struck the Harcar rocks on 7 September 1838. The consequent publicity changed Grace Darling's life and ensured the fame of this part of Northumberland. Nothing, however, can be seen of this wreck or the hundreds of others that occurred amongst these dangerous islands.

THE FARNE ISLANDS

NATURAL HISTORY

The islands have been created nature reserves, administered by the National Trust in collaboration with other bodies. There is a nature trail on Inner Farne, and visitors are requested to follow all rules and instructions given on the islands, with a view to the preservation of their wildlife.

The vegetation is sparse, although as many as seventy flowering plants have been recorded—including elder bushes, introduced by lighthouse men, and a Californian plant, *Amsinckia intermedia*, which has characteristic orange flowers and is thought to have been introduced as poultry feed. Rabbits and rats also are the legacy of generations of lighthouse keepers, and rabbits may still be seen on Brownsman and Staples.

It is the indigenous fauna that is the object of both popular and scientific interest. The Farnes are the only east-coast breeding site for the world's rarest seal—the grey seal. This large seal breeds on Staples and Brownsman, calving in the late autumn. It is a protected animal, although culls have had to take place recently to stop soil erosion on some islands and so preserve them for other members of the islands' wildlife. Any visitor is bound to see large numbers of these curious creatures.

The Farnes are a major site for breeding sea-birds, all the more attractive to the visitor because many species are very tame. Most notable are the eider ducks and puffins which nest on Inner Farne and other islands in their hundreds. Large numbers of breeding cormorants and guillemots are found on the less accessible rocks and islands, while kittiwakes, shags, herring gulls, and four species of tern—arctic, common, roseate and sandwich—are all found nesting in appreciable numbers.

The best time to visit the islands is during the nesting season, from the end of May to early June, when many birds can be seen at very close quarters.

BISHOPS, PRIORS AND CURATES

THE BISHOPS OF LINDISFARNE

Aidan	635–52	Ethelwold	721–40
Finán	652–61	Cynewulf	740–80
Colmán	661–4	Higbald	780–803
Tuda	664–5	Egbert	803–21
Eata	678–85	Heathured	821–30
Cuthbert	685–7	Ecgred	830–45
Eadberht	688–98	Eanbert	845–53
Eadfrid	698–721	Eardulph*	854–900

(*left the island in 875)

THE PRIORS OF HOLY ISLAND

Incomplete before 1324; the years before this date show a prior on the island, while after this date the year of accession is given.

1217 Ralph
1234 William
1241 Thomas
1259 Adam of Newsham
1259 Ralph
1270 John
1272 Richard de Claxton
1275 Nicholas
1281 Ralph
1285 Ralph de Morley
1285 Roger
1285 William de
Middleton
1300 Henry de Luceby
13— Stephen de Houeden
1324 John de Laton
1328 Gilbert de Ellewyk
1350 Michael de Chilton
1350 John de
Goldesburgh
1352 William de
Bamburgh

1356 John de Goldesburgh
1362 Richard de
Bekingham
1364 John de Billesfield
1367 William de
Goldesburgh
1374 Thomas de
Hardwyk
1379 John de Normanby
1381 John de Aclyff
1383 William de Trollop
1383 John de Billesfield
1385 William de Trollop
1391 William de Aslakeby
1394 John de Newburne
1395 William de Aslakeby
1397 Robert Claxton
1401 John de Newburne
1417 John Morys
1430 William Ebchester
1437 Henry Helay
1442 Thomas Ayer

1448 Thomas Worde
1457 Henry Rackett
1458 John de Middleham
1465 John Eden
1472 Thomas Halver
1475 John Aukland
1482 William Rodburne
1487 William Brown and
John Hanby jointly
1590 William Yowdell
1491 John Danby
1492 Galfrid Forest
1501 William Cawthorne
1506 Henry Dalton
1514 Richard Tanfield
1517 Robert Strother
1522 Edward Hyemmers
1525 Henry Thew
1531 John Castell
1536 Thomas Sparke

THE CURATES OF HOLY ISLAND

Early records are incomplete; some names are known only by chance records in documents. Specific dates indicate when a curate takes up office, ie is presented to his parishioners.

Sir John Ainsley	occurs		1544
George Johnson	presented	27 January	1577
John Hilton	presented	29 January	1577
James Forster	presented	20 October	1580
Richard Snawdon	presented	21 July	1582
Bernard Vincent	presented	28 January	1584
Samuel Sinclair	occurs		1591
Christopher Markham	occurs		1601
Samuel Sinclair	occurs		1607
— Hall	buried	21 March	1622
William Mitton	presented	22 Sept	1622
Thomas Panter	occurs		1628
— Lindsey	occurs		1643
Alexander Hewat	buried		1662
John Udney	presented		1667
James Cooper	presented		1695
Alexander Nicolson	presented		1701
James Robertson (father)	presented		1712
James Robertson (son)	presented		1738
Lancelot Wilson	presented		1790
Anthony Watson	presented		1822
J. Horsley Dakyns	presented		1867
W. W. F. Keeling	presented		1876
David Bryson	presented		1893
Irvine Crawshaw	presented		1906
W. Barrick Hall	presented		1919
Robert Davies	presented		1926
Ernest E. C. Elford	presented		1932
John P. Hill	presented		1942
E. N. Gray	presented		1946
W. Harold Broome	presented		1950
Thomas J. Martin	presented		1954
Henry Ball	presented		1958
Denis A. Bill	presented		1964

APPENDIX B

A FLORA OF HOLY ISLAND

This list of plants was collated by Mr M. J. Hudson of the Nature Conservancy Council in 1974. It is arranged in sequence of families, the order being that of most British floras.

PTERIDOPHYTA

Selaginella selaginoides (L.) Link
Equisetum variegatum Schleich.
—*fluviatile* L.
—*palustre* L.
—*arvense* L.
Pteridium aquilinum (L.) Kuhn
Phyllitis scolopendrium (L.) Newn.

Asplenium adiantum-nigrum L.
—*trichomanes* L.
—*ruta-muraria* L.
Dryopteris filix-mas (L.) Schott.
Polypodium vulgare L.
Botrychium lunaria (L.) Sw.

SPERMATOPHYTA

Pinus sylvestris L.

DICOTYLEDONS
Ranunculus acris L.
—*repens* L.
—*bulbosus* L.
—*flammula* L.
—*sceleratus* L.
—*trichophyllus* Chaix
—*aquatilis* L.
Aquilegia vulgaris L.
Thalictrum minus L.

Papaver rhoeas L.
—*dubium* L.

Fumaria capreolata L.
—*officinalis* L.

Sinapis arvensis L.
—*alba* L.
Raphanus raphanistrum L.
Cakile maritima Scop.
Coronopus squamatus (Forsk.) Aschers.
Capsella bursa-pastoris (L.) Medic.
Cochlearia officinalis L.
—*danica* L.
Alyssum alyssoides (L.) L.
Erophila verna (L.) Chevall.
Cardamine pratensis L.
Rorippa nasturtium-aquaticum (L.) Hayek.
—*microphylla* (*Boenn.*) Hyland
Matthiola incana (L.) R. Br.
Hesperis matronalis L.
Cheiranthus cheiri L.
Alliaria petiolata (Bieb.) Cavara & Grande

133

Sisymbrium officinale (L.) Scop.

Reseda luteola L.

Viola odorata L.
—hirta L.
—riviniana Reichb.
—canina L.
—tricolor L.

Polygala vulgaris L.

Helianthemum chamaecistus Mill.

Silene vulgaris (Moench) Garcke
—maritima With.
—noctiflora L.
—dioica (L.) Clairv.
—alba (Mill.) E. H. L. Krause.
Lychnis flos-cuculi L.
Dianthus plumarius L.
Cerastium arvense. L.
—holosteoides Fr.
—glomeratum Thuill
—atrovirens Bab.
—semidecandrum L.
Stellaria media (L.) Vill.
—pallida (Dumort). Piré
Sagina apetala Ard.
—ciliata Fr.
—maritima Don.
—procumbens L.
—nodosa (L.) Fenzl.
Honkenya peploides (L) Ehrh.
Arenaria serpyllifolia L.
—leptoclados (Reichb.) Guss.
—balearica L.
Spergula arvensis L.
Spergularia media (L.) C. Presl.
—marina (L.) Griseb.
Scleranthus annus L.

Montia fontana L.

Chenopodium bonus-henricus L.
—album L.

Chenopodium rubrum L.
Atriplex littoralis L.
—patula L.
—hastata L.
—glabriuscula Edmondst.
—laciniata L.
Halimione portulacoides (L.) Aellen.
Suaeda maritima (L.) Dumort.
Salsola kali L.
Salicornia dolichostachya Moss
—europaea L.

Malva sylvestris L.
—neglecta Wallr.

Linum catharticum L.
Radiola linoides Roth.

Geranium phaeum L.
—sanguineum L.
—dissectum L.
—molle L.
—pusillum L.
—robertianum L.
Erodium cicutarium (L.) L'Hérit.

Acer pseudoplatanus L.

Laburnum anagyroides Medic.
Ulex europeus L.
Ononis repens L.
Medicago sativa L.
—lupulina L.
Melilotus officinalis (L.) Pall.
Trifolium pratense L.
—arvense L.
—striatum L.
—scabrum L.
—hybridum L.
—repens L.
—campestre Schreb.
—dubium Sibth.
Anthyllis vulneraria L.
Lotus corniculatus L.
Astragalus danicus Retz
Vicia hirsuta (L.) Gray

Vicia cracca L.
—sepium L.
—sativa L.
—angustifolia L.
—lathyroides L.
Lathyrus pratensis L.

Filipendula ulmaria (L.) Maxim.
Rubus fruticosus L. sensu lato
Potentilla palustris (L.) Scop.
—sterilis (L.) Garcke
—anserina L.
—reptans L.
Fragaria vesca L.
Geum urbanum L.
Agrimonia eupatoria L.
—odorata (Gouan.) Mill
Alchemilla vulgarus L. sensu lato
Sanguisorba officinalis L.
Poterium sanguisorba L.
Acaena anserinifolia (J.R.&G. Forst.)
    Druce
Rosa pimpinellifolia L.
—rubiginosa L.
Prunus spinosa L.
Cotoneaster horizontalis Decne.
Crataegus monogyna Jacq.

Sedum rosea (L.) Scop.
—anglicum Huds.
—album L.
—acre L.

Saxifraga granulata L.

Parnassia palustris L.

Epilobium hirsutum L.
—parviflorum Schreb.
—montanum L.
—palustre L.
—angustifolium L.
Oenothera erythrosepala Borbás

Myriophyllum spicatum L.

Hippuris vulgaris L.

Callitriche stagnalis
Hydrocotyle vulgaris L.
Chaerophyllum temulentum L.
Anthryiscus caucalis Bieb.
—sylvestris (L.) Hoffm.
Torilis japonica (Hoult.) DC
—nodosa (L.) Gaertn.
Conium maculatum L.
Conopodium majus (Gouan). Loret.
Aegopodium podagraria L.
Oenanthe lachenalii C. C. Gmel.
Foeniculum vulgare Mill.
Ligusticum scoticum L.
Angelica sylvestris L.
Heracleum sphondylium L.
—mantegazzianum Somm. & Levier

Euphorbia helioscopia L.
—peplus L.

Polygonum aviculare L. sensu lato
—raii Bab.
—amphibium L.
—persicaria L.
—convolvulus L.
Rumex acetosella L. sensu lato
—acetosa L.
—crispus L.
—obtusifolia L.

Urtica urens L.
—dioica L.

Betula pendula Roth.
—pubescens Ehrh.
Alnus glutinosa (L.) Gaertn.

Salix viminalis L.
—caprea L.
—aurita L.
—repens L.

Limonium vulgare Mill.
Armeria maritima (Mill.) Willd.

Primula veris L.
—*vulgaris* Huds.
Anagallis tenella (L.) L.
Glaux maritima L.
Samolus valerandi L.

Fraxinus excelsior L.

Centaurium erythraea Rafn.
—*capitatum* (Willd.) Borbás
—*littorale* (D. Turner) Gilmour
Gentianella campestris (L.) Börner
—*amarella* (L.) Börner *sensu lato*

Menyanthes trifoliata L.

Cynoglossum officinale L.
Omphalodes verna Moench.
Symphytum x uplandicum Nyman.
Pentaglottis sempervirens (L.) Tausch.
Lycopsis arvensis L.
Myosotis scorpioides L.
—*caespitosa* K. F. Schultz
—*arvensis* (L.) Hill.
—*ramosissima* Rochel.
Echium vulgare L.

Convolvulus arvensis L.
Calystegia sepium (L.) R. Br.

Lycium chinese Mill.
Hyoscyamus niger L.
Solanum dulcamara L.
Datura stramonium L.

Verbascum thapsus L.
Linaria vulgaris Mill.
Cymbalaria muralis Gaertn., Mey. & Scherb.
Scrophularia nodosa L.
—*umbrosa* Dumort.
Mimulus guttatus DC.
Erinus alpinus L.
Veronica beccabunga L.
—*anagallis-aquatica* L.
—*scutellata* L.

Veronica officinalis L.
—*chamaedrys* L.
—*serpyllifolia* L.
—*arvensis* L.
—*hederifolia* L.
—*persica* Poir.
Rhinanthus minor L.
Euphrasia officinalis L. *sensu lato*
Odontites verna (Bellardi) Dumort.

Orobanche minor Sm.

Pinguicula vulgaris L.

Mentha arvensis L.
—*aquatica* L.
Thymus drucei Ronn.
Salvia verbenaca L.
Prunella vulgaris L.
Stachys palustris L.
Lamium amplexicaule L.
—*moluccellifolium* Fr.
—*purpureum* L.
—*album* L.
Glechoma hederacea L.
Teucrium scorodonia L.
Ajuga reptans L.

Plantago major L.
—*media* L.
—*lanceolata* L.
—*maritima* L.
—*coronopus* L.
Littorella uniflora (L.) Aschers.

Campanula rotundifolia L.

Sherardia arvensis L.
Galium cruciata L. Scop.
—*mollugo* L.
— —*erectum*
—*verum* L.
—*palustre* L.
—*aparine* L.

Sambucus nigra L.

Valerianella locustra (L.) Betcke.
Valeriana officinalis L.
—*dioica* L.
Centranthus ruber (*L.*) DC.

Dipsacus fullonum L.
Knautia arvensis (L.) Coult.

Senecio jacobaea L.
—*sylvaticus* L.
—*vulgaris* L.
Tussilago farfara L.
Pulicaria dysenterica (L.) Bernh.
Solidago virgaurea L.
Astor tripolium L.
—*novae-belgii* L.
Erigeron acer L.
Bellis perennis L.
Eupatorium cannabinum L.
Achillea millefolium L.
Tripleurospermum maritimum (L.) Koch
Matricaria matricarioides (Less.) Porter
Chrysanthemum parthenium (L.) Bernh.
—*vulgare* (L.) Bernh.
Artemisia vulgaris L.
Carlina vulgaris L.
Arctium minus Bernh.
Carduus tenuiflorus Curt.
—*acanthoides* L.
Cirsium vulgare (Savi) Ten.
—*palystre* (L.) Scop.
—*arvense* (L.) Scop.
Centaurea nigra L.
Cichorium intybus L.
Lapsana communis L.
Hypochoeris radicata L.
Leontodon autumnalis L.
—*hispidus* L.
—*taraxacoides* (Vill.) Mérat.
Tragopogon pratensis L.
Sonchus arvensis L.
—*oleraceus* L.
—*asper* (L.) Hill
Hieracium pilosella L.
—*aurantiacum* L.
Crepis capillaris (L.) Wallr.

Taraxacum officinale Weber
—*laevigatum* (Willd.) DC

MONOCOTYLEDONS
Baldellia ranunculoides (L.) Parl.
Alisma plantago-aquatica L.

Triglochin palustris L.
—*maritima* L.

Zostera angustifolia (Hornem.)
Reichb.
—*noltii* Hornem.

Potamogeton natans L.
—*gramineus* L.
—*pectinatus* L.

Endymion non-scriptus (L.) Garcke
Muscari atlanticum Boiss. & Rent.

Juncus gerardii Lois.
Juncus bufonius L.
—*inflexus* L.
—*effusus* L.
—*maritimus* Lam.
—*conglomeratus* L.
—*articulatus* L.
Luzula campestris (L.) DC

Allium oleraceum L.

Iris pseudacorus L.

Epipactis palustris (L.) Crantz
Listera ovata (L.) R. Br.
Coeloglossum viride (L.)
Orchis mascula (L.) L.
Dactylorchis fuchsii (Druce) Vermeul.
—*maculata* (L.) Vermeul.
—*incarnata* (L.) Vermeul.
—*purpurella* (T. & T. A. Stephenson)
Vermeul.
Anacamptis pyramidalis (L.) Rich
Lemna trisulca L.
—*minor* L.

I

Sparganium erectum L.

Eriophorum angustifolium Honck.
—*vaginatum* L.
Scirpus maritimus L.
—*setaceus* L.
Eleocharis quinqueflora (F. X. Hartmann) Schwarz.
—*palustris* (L.) Roem. & Schutt.
Blysmus compressus (L.) Panz. ex Link.
—*rufus* (Huds.) Link.
Schoenus nigricans L.
Carex distans L.
—*demissa* Hornem.
—*serotina* Merat.
—*extensa* Gooden
—*rostrata* Stokes
—*vesicaria* L.
—*acutiformis* Ehrh.
—*panicea* L.
—*flacca* Schreb.
—*hirta* L.
—*caryophyllea* Latourr.
—*nigra* (L.) Reichard
—*otrubae* Podp.
—*disticha* Huds.
—*arenaria* L.
—*disticha* Huds.
—*maritima* Gunn
—*pulicaris* L.

Sieglingia decumbens (L.) Bernh.
Festuca pratensis Huds.
—*rubra* L.
—*ovina* L.
Lolium perenne L.
Puccinellia maritima (Huds.) Parl.
Catapodium rigidum (L.) C. E. Hubbard

Poa annua L.
—*pratensis* L.
—*trivialis* L.
Dactylis glomerata L.
Cynosurus cristatus L.
Briza media L.
Anisantha sterilis (L.) Nevski
Bromus mollis L.
Agropyron repens (L.) Beauvois
—*junceiforme* (A. & D. Löve) A. & D. Löve
Elymus arenarius L.
Hordeum murinum L.
Koeleria cristata (L.) Pers.
Trisetum flavescens Beauv.
Avena sativa L.
Helictotrichon pratense (L.) Pilg.
—*pubescens* (Huds.) Pilg.
Arrhenatherum elatius (L.) Beauv. ex J. & C. Presl.
Holcus lanatus L.
—*mollis* L.
Deschampsia cespitosa (L.) Beauv.
Aira praecox L.
—*caryophyllea* L.
Ammophila arenaria (L.) Link
Ammocalamagrostis baltica (Schrad.) P. Fourn.
Agrostis stolonifera L.
Phleum pratense L.
—*arenarium* L.
Alopecurus pratensis L.
—*geniculatus* L.
Anthoxanthum odoratum L.
Phalaris arundinacea L.
Parapholis strigosa (Dumort) C. E. Hubbard
Nardus stricta L.
Spartina anglica C. E. Hubbard
—*townsendii* H. & J. Groves

APPENDIX C

CHECKLIST OF BIRDS SEEN ON OR NEAR HOLY ISLAND UP TO JULY 1974

Compiled by Mr E. F. Pithers of the Nature Conservancy Council and arranged in the standard or Wetmore order adopted by most handbooks of British birds. All birds ever recorded are included in this list, but early recordings have been reclassified along modern lines.

Black-throated diver
Great northern diver
Red-throated diver
Great crested grebe
Slavonian grebe
Black-necked grebe
Little grebe
Fulmar
Manx shearwater
Balearic shearwater
Great shearwater
Sooty shearwater
Storm petrel
Gannet
Cormorant
Shag
Grey heron
Little egret
Bittern
Spoonbill
Mallard
Teal
Garganey
Blue-winged teal
Gadwall
Wigeon
Pintail
Shoveler
Scaup
Tufted duck
Pochard
Goldeneye

Long-tailed duck
Velvet scoter
Surf scoter
Common scoter
Eider
King eider
Red-breasted merganser
Goosander
Shelduck
Greylag goose
White-fronted goose
Lesser white-fronted goose
Pink-footed goose
Snow goose
Brent goose
Barnacle goose
Canada goose
Red-breasted goose
Mute swan
Whooper swan
Bewick's swan
Buzzard
Rough-legged buzzard
Sparrowhawk
Goshawk
Honey buzzard
Marsh harrier
Hen harrier
Montagu's harrier
Osprey
Peregrine falcon
Merlin

Kestrel
Red-legged partridge
Partridge
Quail
Pheasant
Water rail
Spotted crake
Corncrake
Moorhen
Coot
Oystercatcher
Lapwing
Ringed plover
Kentish plover
Grey plover
Golden plover
Dotterel
Turnstone
Common snipe
Jack snipe
Woodcock
Redshank
Spotted redshank
Greenshank
Knot
Purple sandpiper
Little stint
Curlew
Whimbrel
Black-tailed godwit
Bar-tailed godwit
Green sandpiper
Wood sandpiper
Common sandpiper
Temminck's stint
Pectoral sandpiper
Dunlin
Curlew sandpiper
Sanderling
Buff-breasted sandpiper
Ruff
Avocet
Grey phalarope
Red-necked phalarope
Wilson's phalarope
Great skua

Pomarine skua
Arctic skua
Long-tailed skua
Great black-backed gull
Lesser black-backed gull
Herring gull
Common gull
Glaucous gull
Iceland gull
Mediterranean gull
Little gull
Black-headed gull
Sabine's gull
Kittiwake
Black tern
Common tern
Arctic tern
Roseate tern
Little tern
Sandwich tern
Razorbill
Little auk
Guillemot
Black guillemot
Puffin
Pallas's sandgrouse
Stock dove
Wood pigeon
Turtle dove
Collared dove
Cuckoo
Barn owl
Little owl
Tawny owl
Long-eared owl
Short-eared owl
Nightjar
Swift
Alpine swift
Kingfisher
Hoopoe
Green woodpecker
Great spotted woodpecker
Wryneck
Skylark
Shorelark

Swallow
House martin
Sand martin
Golden oriole
Raven
Carrion crow
Hooded crow
Rook
Jackdaw
Magpie
Jay
Great tit
Blue tit
Coal tit
Marsh tit
Willow tit
Long-tailed tit
Nuthatch
Tree creeper
Wren
Mistle thrush
Fieldfare
Song thrush
Redwing
Ring ouzel
Blackbird
Wheatear
Stonechat
Whinchat
Redstart
Black redstart
Blue-throat
Robin
Grasshopper warbler
Reed warbler
Sedge warbler
Icterine warbler
Blackcap
Barred warbler
Garden warbler
Whitethroat
Lesser whitethroat
Willow warbler
Chiffchaff
Wood warbler

Arctic warbler
Yellow-browed warbler
Goldcrest
Firecrest
Spotted flycatcher
Pied flycatcher
Red-breasted flycatcher
Dunnock
Meadow pipit
Tree pipit
Rock pipit
Pied/white wagtail
Grey wagtail
Yellow wagtail
Citrine wagtail
Grey-headed wagtail
Waxwing
Great grey shrike
Woodchat shrike
Red-backed shrike
Starling
Rose-coloured starling
Hawfinch
Greenfinch
Goldfinch
Siskin
Linnet
Twite
Redpoll
Arctic redpoll
Bullfinch
Scarlet/common rosefinch
Crossbill
Chaffinch
Brambling
Corn bunting
Yellowhammer
Ortolan bunting
Rustic bunting
Little bunting
Reed bunting
Lapland bunting
Snow bunting
House sparrow
Tree sparrow

BIBLIOGRAPHY

ABBREVIATIONS

HBNC: *History of the Berwickshire Naturalists' Club*
PSAN: *Proceedings of the Society of Antiquaries of Newcastle upon Tyne*
TNHS: *Transactions of the Natural History Society of Northumberland, Durham and Newcastle upon Tyne*

ADDLESHAW, G. W. O. *Holy Island or Lindisfarne*. Sunderland, 1957
ASTLEY, H. J. D. 'The early history and associations of Lindisfarne, or Holy Island', *Journal of the British Archaeological Association*, vol 58 (new series vol 8), (1902), 115–28
ASTON, J. 'The Journal', HBNC, 21, (1909–11), 63–107
BEDE. *Venerablis Bedae Historia ecclesiastica gentis Anglorum*. English Historical Society, 1838
BLACKHAL, G. 'A brieffe narration of the services done to three noble ladyes, 1631–49', *Spalding Club*, 42, (1844), 1–224
BLATHERWICK, C. 'Off the beaten track. Holy Island', *Good Words* 32, (1891), 676–83
BOWES, SIR ROBERT. *A book of the state of the Frontiers and Marches between England and Scotland. 1550*. British Museum MS Cotton Titus F13
BRERETON, SIR WILLIAM. 'Notes on a journey through Durham and Northumberland in 1635', *Surtees Society*, 124, (1914), 1–50
BROWN, G. B. *The Arts in Early England*. 1903–37
BROWN, T. (Holy Island Jim) *Holy Island 'Encore' Songster*. Alnwick, 1887
CARRUTHERS, R. G. *Geology of Belford, Holy Island and the Farne Islands, Memoirs of the Geology Survey No 4*. 2nd ed, 1927
COLGRAVE, B. *Two lives of St Cuthbert*. Cambridge, 1940
CRASTER, SIR JOHN. 'Lindisfarne Liqueur', *Newcastle Life*, 4, (Dec 1962)
CROMARTY, C. *The Lindisfarne Story. A Saga of Island Folk*. Newcastle, 1971
———. *Round and About Lindisfarne*. Berwick upon Tweed, 1974
CROSSMAN, L. H. 'History of Holy Island', PSAN, 3 (3rd series), (1909), 285–311

BIBLIOGRAPHY

CROSSMAN, SIR WILLIAM. 'The recent excavations at Holy Island Priory', HBNC, 13 (1892), 225–40
——. 'Chapel of St Cuthbert-in-the-Sea', HBNC, 13, (1892), 241–2
——. 'Holy Island History', PSAN, 7 (new series), (1897), 73–82
DUNLEAVY, G. W. *Colum's other island*. Madison, 1960
ELFORD, E. E. C. *What to see on the Holy Island of Lindisfarne*. Berwick, 1938
——. *A Brief History of the Holy Island of Lindisfarne*. Berwick, 1938
ELLIS, R. *A Medical Guide to Health Resorts of Northumberland, Durham and their Borders*. 1883
FITZGERALD, J. 'I went to Holy Island', *Coming Events in Britain*, (June 1963)
GALLIERS, J. A. *The Geomorphology of Holy Island*.Geography Department Research Paper, Newcastle University, 1970
GIDDINGS, J. W. and RANDALL, B. A. O. 'The palaeomagnetism of the Holy Island Dyke', TNHS, 18, (1971), 177–82
GRAHAM, F. *Lindisfarne or Holy Island*. Newcastle, 1958
GRAHAM, P. A. *Lindisfarne or Holy Island*. 1920
HALLIDAY, W. *Guide to Holy Island—Descriptive and Historical*. Newcastle, 1907
HART, L. *Isle of Saints*. Newcastle, 1954
HECATEUS.'Lindisfarne in the 1960s', *Ushaw Magazine*, 74, (1964) 82–9
HILL, H. *A Guide to the Holy Island of Lindisfarne*. Newcastle, 1962
HOGG, S. 'Post Weichselian history of the North Northumberland Coastal zone', unpublished dissertation, (1972), Department of Geography, University of Durham
HUTCHINSON, W. *The History and Antiquities of the County Palatine of Durham*. Newcastle, 1785–94
JOHNSTON, G. 'Our visit to Holy Island in May 1854', HBNC, 7, (1873), 27–52
KEELING, W. W. F. *Lindisfarne or Holy Island*. Newcastle, 1883
KENNEDY, J. W. *Holy Island: A lenten pilgrimage*. New York, 1958
Lindisfarne National Nature Reserve. Nature Conservancy Council, Newcastle, 1970
MARTIN, T. J. *A Brief History of the Holy Island of Lindisfarne*. Newcastle, 1962
MATHER, J. Y. 'Aspects of the linguistic geography of Scotland', *Scottish Studies*, *13*, (1969), 1–16
MAWER, SIR ALLEN. *The place names of Northumberland and Durham*. Cambridge, 1920
MILLAR, S. C. *The Lindisfarne Gospels*. 1923

NICHOLSON, J. 'Lindisfarne Lures the Tourist', *Financial Times*, (12 Feb 1969)

NOLAN, J. E. H. 'A pilgrimage to Holy Island and the Farnes', *National Geographic Magazine*, (Oct 1952)

OLIVER, S. *Rambles in Northumberland and on the Scottish Border.* 1835

ORDE, P. *Lindisfarne Castle.* National Trust, nd

PARBURY, K. *Saints of Holy Island.* Newcastle, 1970

PATON, W. B. *Celtic Heritage: The story of the English Presbyterian Church on Holy Island.* 1950

PERRY, R. *A Naturalist on Lindisfarne.* 1946

——. 'Life on Holy Island', *Scots Magazine, 52*, (1949), 53–9

——. 'A thousand years of fishing on Holy Island', *Country Life*, 105, (1949), 322–5

PEVSNER, SIR NICHOLAS. *Northumberland.* 1957

PORTER, J. *The Pastor's Fireside—a novel.* 1817

RAINE, J. *The History and Antiquities of North Durham.* 1852

RANDALL, B. A. C. *et alia.* 'Holy Island Dyke', TNHS, 17, (1970), 127–35

SAVILL, P. 'Holy Island', *Go* (Sept 1962)

SELBY, J. S. D. 'On the foundations of ancient buildings and coins of the Saxon kingdom of Northumbria recently found at Holy Island', HBNC, 2, (1842–9), 159–63

SKELLY, G. *A Guide to Lindisfarne and etc.* Alnwick, 1888

SMITH, C. 'The story of Presbyterians on Holy Island', *Journal of the Presbyterian Historical Society*, 4, (1928–31), 153–63

SOWERBUTTS, D. L. 'Holy Island, Northumberland; a bibliography', unpublished thesis, (1966), London University

TEGNER, H. *The Magic of Holy Island.* Newcastle, 1969

THOMAS, A. C. *The Early Christian Archaeology of North Britain.* 1971

THOMPSON, A. H. *Lindisfarne Priory, Northumberland.* 1949

TOMLINSON, W. W. *Comprehensive Guide to the County of Northumberland.* 1888

——. *Life in Northumberland and Durham during the Sixteenth Century.* 1897

TOOLEY, M. J. 'Lindisfarne Castle Garden—Gertrude Jekyll', unpublished report, (1972), Department of Geography, Durham University

WILSON, F. R. *An Architectural Survey of the churches in the Archdeaconry of Lindisfarne in the County of Northumberland.* Newcastle, 1870

WINCH, N. J. 'Remarks on the geology of Lindisfarne or Holy Island', *Annals of Philosophy*, series 2 vol 4, (1822), 420–34

ACKNOWLEDGEMENTS

MANY people have assisted in the preparation of this book over the last few years. Most especially we should like to record our appreciation for the help and encouragement given to us by the Reverend and Mrs Denis Bill, the vicar and the district nurse of Holy Island. Numerous other people, on and off the island, have given us assistance and information. We are only sorry that it is not possible to mention everyone by name, or to include all the data they gave us. Acknowledgement is due to: Area Medical Officer, Alnwick; Borough of Berwick upon Tweed, Department of the Environment; British Library; British Rail, Eastern Region; County of Northumberland, Social Services Department; Department of Palaeography and Diplomatic, University of Durham; Department of the Environment; Director of Education for Northumberland; Durham County Record Office; Fire Brigade, Morpeth; General Post Office, Postal Services, Morpeth; General Post Office, Telephone Services, Newcastle; Harold Hill & Co Ltd; Customs and Excise, Newcastle; Institute of Geological Sciences; Ministry of Agriculture, Fisheries and Food; Newcastle and Gateshead Water Company; Newcastle Weather Centre; Northumberland Ambulance Services; Northumberland County Records Office; Northumberland County Surveyor; Northumberland River Authority; Northumberland Sea Fisheries Committee; Planning Department, County of Northumberland; Royal Air Force, Acklington; Royal National Lifeboat Institute; South of Scotland Electricity Board; The National Trust; The Northumberland Constabulary; The Royal Commission on Historical Manuscripts; White Fish Authority, South Shields.

For permission to use drawings already published elsewhere and to quote from books, we would like to thank: The Natural History Society of Northumberland, Durham and Newcastle upon Tyne; Department of Geography, Newcastle University; Department of Surveying, Newcastle University; University Library, Newcastle University; Oxford University Press; British Museum, Department of Manuscripts; British Library, Map Room; Northumberland County Records Office; Stafford County Records Office; Dr M. Tooley; Dr J. Galliers; Dr A. C. Thomas; Mr R. Perry; Mr H. Tegner, Dr B. Randall.

A great deal of work went into the collation of an up to date set of island check lists of a wide variety of flora and fauna. It was not possible to include all this material, but we would like to especially thank Mr Eric Pithers, Mr Ian Armstrong and Dr G. Swan for their efforts in this respect. The Nature Conservancy Council, through their local officer, M. J. Hudson, initiated the collation of these lists, which it is hoped will be valuable in other respects.

The following individuals have also been of assistance in producing this book: Rev A. Bickerstaff; Mr M. Briggs; Miss R. Chisholm and her pupils; Rev Fr J. Corrigan; Mr G. Craig; Mr R. Cromarty; Col H. Crossman; Mr R. Dennis; Rev Fr G. Gaughan; Mr J. Hargreaves; Dr M. Hornung; Mr F. Markwell; Dr J. Mather; Miss K. Milton; Mr D. A. O'Connor; Mr A. Piper; Dr B. Roberts; Mr G. Sanderson; Dr S. Sanderson; Mr M. Smith; Mr D. Sowerbutts; Rev Fr J. Tumney.

Finally, we are grateful to the following for permission to reproduce the illustrations in this book. Unacknowledged illustrations are the author's property.

PLATES

Aerofilms Ltd: p 49 (above)
Airviews Ltd, Manchester Airport: pp 50, 67 (above)
Bill, Rev D.: p 85 (below)

ACKNOWLEDGEMENTS

Crown Copyright, reproduced by permission of the Controller of Her Majesty's Stationery Office: p 104
Evening Chronicle, Newcastle upon Tyne: p 103
Grey, Mr Melvin: pp 49, 68, 86 (below)
Northumberland Gazette: p 50 (below)
Purvis, Miss M.: p 85 (above)
Smith, Mr D. M.: p 68 (above)

DIAGRAMS

Crown copyright, reproduced by permission of the Controller of Her Majesty's Stationery Office: p 65
Geography Department, University of Newcastle upon Tyne: pp 20, 25
Natural History Society of Northumberland: p 23
Surveying Department, University of Newcastle upon Tyne: p 10
Thomas, A. C.: p 56

INDEX

148

INDEX

INDEX